The Railways of Richmond upon Thames

By Tim Sherwood

Contents

© 1991

Published by

Forge Books, 55 Brookside,

Wokingham, Berks. RG11 2ST

Typeset and Printed by

Penwell Print Ltd., Kelly Bray, Callington, Cornwall.

Early scenes on the railways to Richmond as recorded by the Illustrated London News: above the Wandle Viaduct at Wandsworth (1 August 1846) and below the Thames bridge at Richmond (21 October 1848).

Part I
Origins and Promotion of Richmond's First Railway: 1830-1846

"... the prettiest place within miles of London ..." [1]

With the success of the Liverpool and Manchester Railway in 1830 numerous schemes for steam locomotive railways were proposed, many of which were in Southern England. Two local schemes in the London area actually succeeded; the London and Greenwich in 1836, and the London and Blackwall in 1840. Most projects were unable to attract capital. One proposal in the early 1830s was a London to Falmouth Railway, which would have passed close to Richmond; similarly a London to Exeter line of 1836 would have affected Richmond. In that year a scheme called the City of London and Richmond was also floated, and addressed the investing public thus:

> "The directors have the pleasure to acquaint the subscribers that the whole of the Parliamentary Plans, Sections, and Books of Reference etc. are completed. The owners, lessees, and occupiers of lands and tenements on the line of the proposed railway are requested to make immediate application to the Director, at the offices of the Company (by letter), for any number of shares they may require ..."

> Jonas Binns
> 10 Mansion House St.
> November 10 1836 [2]

The Adelphi Theatre advertised a playbill with a bird's eye view of its intended route: a copy of this, showing the railway on a viaduct for most of its route (probably because the London and Greenwich was), survives. [3]

The Vestry at Mortlake, "once a handsome riverside village" [4] were alarmed at this scheme, giving cogent reasons for opposing the project at their meeting on 20 January 1837:

> " – because the inhabitants, either collectively or individually (even if the railway was completed) would not derive the smallest benefit
> – that the most serious annoyance would be experienced by obstructing highways and footpaths
> – that it would be a needless and uncalled for invasion of private property and cause an irreparable injury to houses and lands of several inhabitants
> – no advantage as there is no manufacturing or object of commerce along the whole route to be benefited
> – that if completed it would lead to the increase of desecration of the Lord's day in the neighbourhood." [5]

An illustration of the proposed terminus in Richmond is also in existence; [6] it would have been a lavish and handsome building had it been possible to finance it. It is probable that other unlikely schemes were floated in the early 1840s, as the railway 'mania' gained momentum.

In 1844 a prospectus was issued for the "Richmond and West End Junction" railway, and was the first proposal to have support from within the railway industry – from the London and South Western Railway Company (LSWR). The details of the proposed company were: paid up capital £500,00 in 25,000 shares of £20, with a provisional managing committee of twenty-six members, of whom nine came from Richmond. One was the Hon. C.P. Villiers, MP for the town. The other members are listed in Appendix A. The surveyor was William Chadwick, who subsequently became company Chairman; the Engineer was George Parker Bidder, an associate of Robert Stephenson. The scheme therefore had a look of respectability and realism, for it was to use the LSWR line from Battersea as a means of entering London. The title "West End Junction" referred to the extension that would be constructed from outside the LSWR's Nine Elms terminus, through Vauxhall, to the south end of Hungerford/Waterloo Bridge, approximately where Charing Cross railway bridge now is. Somewhat ambitiously the prospectus states that the line would be extended over the river into Hungerford Market. It was hoped, but it could have been no more than a hope, to site the terminus on the north bank of the Thames; the prospectus was designed to entice investors. It was something for the future because a railway bridge was not built here until Charing Cross station was opened by the South Eastern Railway (SER) in 1864. Worth recording, however, is the fact that the Richmond Company were the first to publicly propose a terminus at Waterloo, which provided the impetus for the LSWR to move from Nine Elms, which was inaccessible and small. Proposed also at this time was a branch from the Richmond Railway to Kew Bridge and Brentford. As will be seen, this was a realistic and practicable proposition.

The prospectus also gave information about stage and omnibus services between Richmond and London, which throws some light on travel and mobility in the pre-railway age. Both nationally and locally road passenger services increased in the 1820s and 1830s; there had been six coaches running between Richmond and London in 1825, each coach doing two return journeys, and Wimbledon had only one coach which did two return journeys. [7] An omnibus called "Pilot" started running from Richmond to London, via Putney, in 1830. There were ten omnibuses and short-stages by 1838-9, five of which ran from Richmond to the Bank, and five to St Paul's. [8]

By 1840, coach and omnibus services had expanded significantly around most big towns, so that from the Post Office Directory of 1843 it can be seen that coaches to and from Richmond originated from ten different points in London. Similarly, carts and carriers' waggons left for Richmond from no less than twenty-two inns. There were two steamboat services, and barges sailed from the Bull Wharf. Some historians aver that the first steamboat operated commercially on the Thames was 'The Richmond' owned by a Mr Dawson and put into service between Richmond and London experimentally in 1813.

A survey of the same year, carried out by the promoters of the railway, exaggerated the position: it said that seventeen coaches were working between Richmond and London, each carrying eighteen passengers, and performing a total of 686 journeys per week. This produced a total of 1,180,608 passengers in a year. The survey also stated that for twenty four weeks of the year six steamboats carried an average of twenty passengers each to London; the yearly total was calculated as 33,600, which, when added to the coach and bus passengers totalled 1,214,208. The Prospectus, always optimistic, concluded that this number could be doubled "as is usual in estimated railway traffic". Apparently with parcels this would produce a revenue of £59,066.12s 9d per year, which "on a capital of £500,000 is rather more than 11%". Most investors would have treated these figures cautiously, as promoters always inflated potential traffic.

Although Richmond was described in 1840 as a ". . . place of trifling thoroughfare, and . . . no manufactories" [9] much goods and freight was conveyed by carriers' waggon and river barge; probably seven per day of the former, and four per day of the latter, with services growing rapidly within the next few years. The wagons and boats were owned by three firms: William Bell, Cripps and Ackland, and T.C. Godfrey. Not only were there passenger services to London, but coaches and buses ran to Kingston, Hampton Court and Twickenham.

In the event a modest railway scheme was presented to Parliament: the extension to Hungerford/Waterloo bridge was omitted because as a result of negotiations it was agreed that the LSWR would build it, whilst the Richmond company would build a line from the LSWR at Battersea to Richmond. However, a rival scheme had appeared called the "South London and Windsor" railway, following a similar route through Putney and Mortlake. In its admirably clear and brief Report[10] of 1845 on railway proposals in the London area, the Board of Trade* said of this project:

---

* Because so many schemes were being proposed at this time, the Railway Department of the Board of Trade was filtering them for Parliament.

RICHMOND OLD STATION

A mid <u>1860's</u> view of the up platform (top) and (left) an up train from Windsor to Waterloo approaching behind William Adams' radial tank engine, the main motive power of South Western suburban services in the closing years of the last century. Below – a train bound for Windsor enters the station under Church Road bridge.

"This scheme wears such an aspect of extravagance upon its face, that it is difficult to conceive upon what prospect of profit it can have been put forward. We consider that there are public grounds why it should not receive the sanction of Parliament". However, of the Richmond (and formerly West End Junction) the Report was favourable: ". . . a very advantageous outlet will be provided for the population of London to places of favourite resort, while accommodation will be given to a considerable local traffic already existing between the many populous villages along the line and London". As expected this scheme was supported by the LSWR in the Parliamentary Committee hearings, which was crucial. It was opposed by those interests which would be adversely affected, for example, the Fulham and Putney Bridge Company, the Hammersmith Bridge Company, and the Surrey Iron Railway. Also opposing were the Parishes of Putney who said the scheme would be neither productive nor beneficial, and Mortlake, presumably on much the same grounds as nine years before, though Richmond Vestry supported the Bill. It is likely that there was opposition from the steamboat owners, the coaching and the omnibus interest, and the carriers, but there is no surviving record of this. A petition opposing was submitted by the inhabitants of Mortlake to the House of Commons Committee.† Earl Spencer, Lord of the Manor, supported the scheme, and sold land on Putney Common at profit to himself.

In his evidence for the Bill, [11] the LSWR Chairman, William Chaplin (who had been a coach owner) estimated the number of passengers travelling from Richmond to London as follows: "767,104 passengers by land omnibus and about 96,000 by water . . . and in addition to that about 40,000 from Putney and Wandsworth in the winter, and 67,000 in the summer". Once again, the figures are probably exaggerated. For the railway, Chaplin proposed a single fare of 9d, which he said was half the coach fare, and which he hoped would yield £35,082. Interestingly he said the railway would not attempt to compete with the river for heavy goods traffic: by and large, the national experience to that date was different, but some heavy goods, for example, sand and bricks, continued to be brought to Richmond by river well into the twentieth century. Chapman also said that the river journey could take five hours from central London, depending on the tide, which he considered to be "too tedious" for businessmen. Evidence given on omnibus services suggests that the route to London was over Kew Bridge and via Hammersmith (or over Hammersmith Bridge following the route of the present no. 9 bus). It was stated in evidence that the Richmond bus was no longer using Putney Bridge, though as already noted, it is probable that some coaches and omnibuses went through Putney, the precursors of the present no. 37 bus route.

The information given in evidence was similar to that in the prospectus – the same survey had been used – except that it was stated that the omnibuses carried eight passengers in winter, and twelve in summer. This sounds more likely than the previous figure of eighteen. The journey to Richmond took 1 ½ hours. It was pointed out that people would cross the bridge from Fulham to Putney to catch a train, there being "very few" buses crossing (probably because of the toll), except for the Wimbledon service.

But what was the reaction in Richmond to the proposed railway? As already noted, the Vestry supported the project. A witness at the Parliamentary hearing stated that rents had diminished in Richmond, and that the general feeling in the town was in favour of the railway (but this might have been an absentee landlord); the principal public anxiety was over the number of roads to be crossed. But there is evidence that there was much consternation; a recent writer has said:

> "Richmond at the mere idea was panic stricken. The inhabitants were as
> alarmed as they would be today if an atomic plant were to be built in the Terrace
> Gardens. In the Georgian houses of Richmond, in the sedate drawing rooms and
> in the parlours of the prosperous tradespeople, there was talk of nothing else". [12]

A memorandum was circulated in 1844, pointing out that the promoters of the line did not live in Richmond. This circular obtained only 72 signatures even though the opposition felt that "Richmond's high character for respectability would be destroyed as well as sending away those fam-

---

† This no longer survives; most of the House of Commons records and Minutes of Evidence etc. were destroyed by bombing in the Second World War.

ilies of distinction who were its principal support". [13] Other families and individuals may not have felt so threatened, and may have perceived the railway as an opportunity for social change and economic growth. As always, what the poorer people thought is not recorded. But the problems were real and the fears prophetic; it was anticipated that Richmond would become an "outgrowth of London" [14] even though it was an "exclusive small town and the inhabitants were not in the habit of going daily to London for reasons of business". [15]

Nevertheless it was realised by others that the line coming in from the east to Kew Road would need to demolish little property, and then, as now, property was a telling factor. The Bill passed through both Houses of Parliament and received the Royal Assent on 21 July 1845 (at the height of the railway 'mania') incorporating the Richmond Railway Company with a capital of £260,000 and the usual powers of compulsory purchase. Legal and Parliamentary expenses had amounted to only £3,892 8s 3d, described by the Times as "trifling".

THE CONSTRUCTION AND OPENING OF THE RAILWAY

At the same time in July 1845 the LSWR obtained their Act to build their 'Metropolitan Extension', as they called it, from Vauxhall to Hungerford/Waterloo Bridge. The Engineer for this was Joseph Locke, who had taken over the construction of the London and Southampton line in 1837, and who had also been appointed to the Richmond line. G.P. Bidder had dropped out for unknown reasons. Locke was one of the great early railway engineers, and in tribute when he died in 1860, the 'Times' obituary said that Robert Stephenson, Brunel and Locke had formed the Triumvirate of the Engineering World. As already noted, the Richmond line diverged from the Southampton line at Falcon Bridge in Battersea (later to become Clapham Junction), where enough land had been bought on which to build a station (more of this later). The first station was at Wandsworth, the next at Putney, then Barnes, and then Mortlake. The Directors had decided that Putney and Barnes stations, like Nine Elms, should be elegant as well as functional, for they minuted in March 1846 "The suggestion be offered to the Surveyor to have tiles for the roof (sic) instead of slates, chimney tops in character and a small room in the roof". The contractor for the engineering and earthworks was Henry Knill who was awarded a contract for £50,000 which was accepted on 12th September 1845. In March 1846 a tender from John Tombs (who must have been another local builder) for £11,075 was accepted for the two stations. Sadly, only Barnes survives as an example of a station on this line in anything like its original form: neo-Tudor and "red brick with diapering" [16] and probably one of the earliest surviving stations in the Greater London area. The architect was Sir William Tite, who had also built Nine Elms.

Nine Elms was demolished to make way for the New Covent Garden Market, opened in 1974. In 1952 Sir John Betjeman had called it a complete early station survival, part of the Georgian Age, classic and stuccoed. Such stations, he had written, are ". . . stately but not sumptuous. They are spreading but not soaring. They suggest coaches pulled by iron horses. They are merely another sort of posting inn . . .". This was in his book "First and Last Loves". Similarly, Professor White has written, in the "Railways of Southern England", that the simple classical style of Nine Elms reminds us that ". . . the Age of Elegance survived in to the Railway Age". Finally, Cherry and Pevsner, in "London 2: South", describe it thus: "a quietly Italian front of seven bays, the centre five opened up in a giant loggia of pillars and arches beneath a straight attic: a sound job without the dramatisation of Euston".

It only served Richmond for two years, the success of the Richmond line rendering it inadequate. It was superseded by Waterloo in 1848, which until rebuilt in the early Twentieth century, was architecturally negligible, and a hideous muddle for the passenger. Sir William Tite also built Southampton Terminus (which is no longer a station, but is a listed building), and Windsor and Eton Riverside, which also survives, as a working station, and for which Barnes may have been a forerunner.

Sir George Larpent of Putney obtained compensation for his land situated to the east of Putney station. He took the Company to Arbitration and obtained £7250 for his house, and £900 per acre for his land. [17] He had been a member of the Provisional Committee of the Richmond and West End

A very early view of a LSWR train for Ludgate Hill headed by a Beattie well-tank, with North London carriages on the right.

A Metropolitan train bound for Aldgate via the Hammersmith and City line. A new platform has been added and there is now a footpath linking Church Road with the station.

Possibly dating from the same time as the previous photograph, this view shows a LSWR train via Addison Road with an Adams 'radial' tank engine and a District train for Mansion House with 4-4-0 tank No. 9.

A South Western train from Kingston to Waterloo leaves Richmond Old Station whilst an Adams T1 class 0-4-4 tank stands in the New Station with a rake of six-wheeled carriages bound for Waterloo via Addison Road. The New Station has conductor rails for District Railway electric trains.

Junction Railway, but must have dropped out.

At Barnes the railway was obliged by its Act to build an overbridge to carry the Hammersmith Bridge Company's road over the line. On completion this bridge was described, in a letter to the Times, as "steep and ugly", disfiguring the Common, it was alleged. The writer complained that the bridge was "covered with a deep layer of loose unbinding pebbles – almost impassable for one horse vehicles". At Mortlake, after a dispute over the Church path the company offered to build an over-bridge at the station, but this was rejected by the Vestry. [18] They disagreed over the width of the bridge. However, the level crossings were not popular, with some people, as a letter to The Times shows:

> "Sir – Those in the habit of going to Richmond through East Sheen are in con-
> stant danger, owing to this line passing directly across the public high road.
> There are gates, it is true, but they are most carelessly guarded. On Saturday
> last, within a minute after the Sunbury coach, with six passengers inside and
> eighteen outside, had passed over the rail, a train came along at full speed.
> General Pasley (Inspector of Railways) will most likely look to the safety of the
> public after some awful accident has occurred. Some great neglect must have
> happened, or Parliament would never have allowed the Company to pass direct-
> ly over a frequented road, with scarcely any protection for the public. They ought
> to have been compelled to make a bridge over the line. Trusting you will give this
> a place in your valuable paper and that the effect will be that a proper remedy
> will be found.
>
> I am, Sir, your obedient servant,
> ONE OF THE PUBLIC
> London, June 29"

Delay occurred at the Richmond station site over negotations with Messrs George Robinson and John Carrell, who owned houses and gardens at this spot.

The line cost £195,000, or roughly £30,000 a mile, most of which was absorbed in land purchase, as with other railways. It was completed in nine months; it was unusual for a railway to cost less than estimated, and to be completed early. The only engineering works of significance were the viaduct over the Wandle and the Surrey Iron Railway, and the cutting at Putney, splitting the estate of Sir George Larpent. As the Railway Chronicle Travelling Chart, published at this time for the guidance of travellers, said: ". . . the works have been light, and have given no opportunity for the display of engineering skill". How Joseph Locke felt about that is not recorded.

On Friday 18 July 1846 the Directors accompanied General Pasley on his inspection of the line; his only criticism was that the level crossing gates between Barnes and Richmond should be length-ened to prevent cattle wandering on to the line. Otherwise, the line could be opened to the public on Monday 27 July.

A ceremonial opening was held on Wednesday 22 July. A sixteen coach train for the Directors and their guests, hauled by the locomotive 'Crescent', left Nine Elms and proceeded gently to Richmond where a triumphal arch had been erected in front of the uncompleted station. An eyewitness has recorded an account of the scene:

> "There was naturally a considerable amount of excitement pervading the town
> on that occasion, and a most imposing sight it certainly was to see the first train
> approaching the station, gracefully turning round the curved line of rails which
> existed with the first old station, about 200 yards from the platform, with the
> Royal Standard flying from the fore part of the Engine to which it was attached,
> and a fine band of music accompanying the train." [19]

Church bells were rung, and a meal for 300 was provided at the Castle Hotel, at which suitable toasts and speeches were made. Meanwhile, free trips to Nine Elms were offered to the public, to which there must have been an enthusiastic response. There was something to celebrate; the rail-way had arrived, and steam locomotive railways were changing the relationship between time and space.

Describing the line from its junction with the Southampton line at Falcon Bridge, Battersea, the "Illustrated London News" said:

> "It then pursues a pretty course through the villas, orchards, and nursery gardens, which stud the locality, till it reaches Wandsworth. The River Wandle and the valley are crossed by a splendid viaduct of 22 arches, three of which are 70 feet span, the entire length of the work being about 1,000 feet. Leaving Wandsorth Station we have for a moment a picturesque peep at the Thames, and the line pursues a course through a deep cutting of some extent, until it reaches Putney, where it proceeds over the level country to Barnes Common, which is crosses. Mortlake is the next point of notice, and here a very elegant station is nearly completed. The remainder of the course is through fields and gardens, passing a little to the south of the grounds of Kew, on to the terminus in the Kew-Road at Richmond, where a plain, but spacious station is in course of erection."
> [20]

Richmond Station was at the most convenient location – given the company's desire to avoid demolishing houses (to forestall opposition and save themselves expense). "Herepath", later styled the "Railway Magazine", said it had the merit of being close to the town centre. Although the station was uncompleted, the company was anxious to catch the summer traffic.

Another description, with a biblical touch, was not so complimentary:

> ". . . while the country generally and that at the terminus in particular is remarkable for beauty, the part through which the line passes is extremely wanting in the picturesque . . . out of evil cometh good". [21]

A Mr Cooper was Richmond's first station master, appointed from the opening of the line. He must have been popular and respected because three years later, in July 1849, he was formally presented with a silver snuff box and purse containing £36.10s, being:

> ". . . the residue of a subscription raised by the inhabitants of Richmond and its vicinity (for the) uniform and unceasing attention paid by him to all classes in the performance of his duties as Superintendent of the station at Richmond". [22]

In the list of subscribers were the ex-King and Queen of France (Louis Philippe had abdicated in the 1848 Revolution, and visited Richmond), and Lord John Russell. [23]

It had been agreed in August 1845 that the LSWR would work the line at their own expense, paying the Richmond Company two-thirds of revenue, which would be re-negotiated when the extension to Waterloo Bridge was opened. Negotiations had begun, before the opening, for a merger with the LSWR. But terms had been delayed by the success of the line; by the end of 1846 Richmond Railway Company shares were rising, whilst LSWR shares had gone into one of their periodic declines, aggravated on this occasion by the economic depression. The Richmond Company were in a stronger bargaining position; receipts would be even better when the extension to Waterloo was opened, and also when the line was extended westwards to Staines and Windsor.

Provisional terms in July 1846 consisted of an offer to convert £195,000 worth of paid-up Richmond stock into LSWR stock, after paying construction expenses, with dividends, payable from January 1847. But no arrangement was made for a Richmond director to have a seat on the LSWR Board. This deal was considered to be unreasonable, and the Railway Times recommended shareholders to refuse. As a result the representative of this journal had not been invited to the opening ceremony. Richmond shareholders were able to extract a better bargain from the LSWR:- a choice of three £15 Richmond shares or one £50 Richmond share with 5% interest payable from July to January. Also, a Richmond director would join the LSWR Board, though difficulties arose because no vacancy was available. T.B. Simpson, the Richmond Deputy Chairman was nominated and the merger was completed in January 1847.

At the start, the service from Nine Elms was seventeen trains per day, replacing, according to the Chairman, 98 horse buses, with fares at 1s 4d (7p) first class, 1s 0d (5p) second, and 8d (3½p) third. Fast trains, with no third class accommodation, would have a premium of 2d. The ILN, which had a social conscience, said "we must confess we should like to see the third class fare reduced to 6d

(2½p). The directors, no doubt, contemplate this, as one of their boons to the people". Likewise, Herepath said the fares were too high, given that passengers had to spend another 4d (2p) on the steamboat from Nine Elms to London. Whenever the LSWR were to open or operate a line they were criticised over the level of fares, and on this occasion they were reduced to 1s, 10d, and 6d. But nevertheless, railway fares were high as a general rule, and until the last quarter of the nineteenth century, prevented many people from travelling by rail.

One historical significance of the Richmond Railway is that it prompted the LSWR to move their London terminus from Nine Elms, which could only be reached by boat or by bus, to Waterloo Bridge. The LSWR may have considered extending the line over the river to Hungerford Market (where Charing Cross station now stands). Originally the Richmond Company did, sending their plans to the LSWR, who offered to subscribe £100,000 towards the cost. Once the railway at Richmond was constructed it quickly led to the provision of further railways up the Thames Valley, namely, the extension to Staines and Windsor, and the Hounslow loop branching off at Barnes. The junction in Battersea where the Richmond line branches away from the main Southampton line, formed the nodal point for other junctions, eventually becoming Clapham Junction. The LSWR were reluctant to build a station here, but the Richmond Company had wanted one so that passengers from Richmond could get to Southampton and the West of England without going into Waterloo.

Notes and References

1.   Simpson's Guide to Richmond, 1888, p.5. Richmond Local Studies Library (R.Lib).
2.   M.S. Ref. L385. 1 RA (R.Lib).
3.   L.385. 1 RA (R.Lib).
4.   B. Cherry & N. Pevsner, The Buildings of England, London 2: South, 1983, p.513.
5.   M.S. 20 Jan 1837 Meeting of Mortlake Vestry ref. L385. 1 RA (R.Lib).
6.   L.385. 1 RA (R.Lib).
7.   Corporation of London Records Office, B.12.V, quoted by T.C. Barker and Michael Robbins, A History of London Transport, vol. 1, 1975, p.392.
8.   Robson's London Directory for 1839, quoted by Barker and Robbins, op.cit., pp.401-2.
9.   Pigot's Directory, 1840, p.639 (R.Lib).
10. Report from the Board of Trade on schemes for facilitating the approach to the Metropolis, 1845 (R.Lib).
11. Minutes and Evidence House of Commons Committee, Richmond Railway Bill, 21 July 1845, House of Lords Record Office (HLRO).
12. M.G. Aldred in Richmond and Twickenham Times (RTT), 11 December 1954.
13, 14, 15. Ibid.
16. Cherry and Pevsner, op.cit., p.469.
17. Minutes, Board of Directors, Richmond Railway Co., Public Record Office (PRO).
18. Stated verbally by Michael Robbins.
19. Hiscoke and Sons Richmond Notes, no.12, January 1864, p.6.
20. Illustrated London News, no date, quoted by Richmond Herald (RH) 27 July 1946.
21. Herepath, 25 July 1846, p.900.
22. Railway Times, 7 July 1849, p.680.
23. Ibid.

Part II
Consolidation and Expansion:
The Railway in the Upper Thames Valley: 1846-1869

"This Railway and its Branches communicate . . . with the suburbs of London celebrated for their picturesque beauty, viz., Richmond, Windsor, Kew, and the Valley of the Thames . . ." [1]

The regular service from Richmond to Nine Elms opened on Monday 27 July 1846 and although the first train from Richmond at 7.45am carried only five passengers in second class, traffic increased rapidly and by 1847 the railway was carrying as many as 25,000 passengers a month. [2] By 1850 there were twenty trains a day. In order to cope with the growth of traffic more tracks had to be provided between Falcon Bridge junction and Nine Elms junction; in 1848 an additional "up" line was opened, and some years later, in 1860, a further "down" line was provided. Most of this extra traffic came from Richmond and the Thames Valley west of Richmond, to which we should now give some consideration.

The promotion and construction of the railway from Richmond to the upper Thames Valley followed consequentially upon the successful promotion and opening of the line from Nine Elms to Richmond. It will be recalled that the 1845 Board of Trade Report [3] had alluded favourably to the extension of the railway west of Richmond, a Prospectus for a 10 mile line from Richmond to Staines having appeared in 1844. This received the support of the Richmond Company directors as it would improve their company's position.

Other towns such as Brentford, Isleworth, and Hounslow, let alone Staines and Windsor, were wanting railway facilities by the mid 1840s. As a result of the opening of the London to Southampton and the London to Bristol lines in 1840, they had lost trade with the decline of the West of England coaches. Furthermore:

"The Thames Valley . . . already held small towns or villages which were popular resorts for Londoners, and only needed a convenient train service to convert them into residential suburbs for business people of the wealthier classes". [4]

No expensive engineering works would be needed and the area was ideal terrain for railway construction, as already noted. Thus by 1846 there were five schemes being floated:

1. Great Western Railway (GWR) Broad Gauge line to Staines, from their London-Bristol line at Ealing.
2. London and Windsor.
3. London, Hounslow and Western.
4. Windsor, Slough and Staines Atmospheric Railway.
5. Staines and Richmond Junction – referred to above.

Numbers 2, 3 and 4 were independently promoted. Number 5, which was the soundest, and would have made an "end-on" junction with the Richmond Railway, was opposed by Richmond Vestry, and the Commissioner of Woods and Forests, the latter:

". . . causing the promoters much unnecessary delay and expense by being unable to make up their minds, that authority finally demanded the substitution of a tunnel for the bridge". [5]

This major alteration would have required more capital, and changes to the Deposited Plans; the Bill was invalidated under Standing Orders. Therefore when the line from Nine Elms to Richmond opened in 1846, no progress had been made in extending it westwards.

ANNO DUODECIMO & DECIMO TERTIO

VICTORIÆ REGINÆ.

****

Cap. xxxiv.

An Act for enabling the *Windsor, Staines, and South-western* (*Richmond* to *Windsor*) Railway Company to make an Extension of their Railway to the Town of *New Windsor ;* and for other Purposes.
[26th *June* 1849.]

WHEREAS an Act was passed in the Session of Parliament held in the Tenth and Eleventh Years of the Reign of Her present Majesty, called " The *Windsor, Staines, and South-western* Railway Act (No. 1.), 1847," whereby the *Windsor, Staines, and South-western* (*Richmond* to *Windsor*) Railway Company were authorized to make a Railway from *Richmond* to *Windsor*, with a Loop Line through *Brentford* and *Hounslow*, and the *London and South-western* Railway Company were empowered to subscribe towards and to accept a Lease or Transfer thereof : And whereas an Act was passed in the last Session of Parliament, called " The *Windsor and South-western* Railway Deviations Act, 1848," whereby the said *Windsor, Staines, and South-western* (*Richmond* to *Windsor*) Railway Company were authorized to make certain Deviations in the Line of the said Railway from *Richmond* to *Windsor:* And whereas it would be of public Advantage that the said Company should be enabled to make an Extension of the said *Windsor, Staines, and South-western* (*Richmond* to *Windsor*) Railway from the authorized Terminus thereof in the Parish of *Datchet* in the County of *Buckingham* into the Town of

margin note: 10 & 11 Vict. c. 58.

margin note: 11 & 12 Vict. c. 75.

[*Local.*]   6 D   *New*

The other schemes are not without interest; the London and Windsor was to run from Pimlico (where Victoria station now is) to Brentford, Colnbrook, Datchet and Windsor. But it planned to cross London streets on the level, so:

> ". . . it received its quietus at the hands of the Commons Committee, nor was it above reproach on its financial side." [6]

The London, Hounslow and Western started from the LSWR at Battersea, and ran via Fulham, Hammersmith, Chiswick, and Brentford to Staines. This also failed in Parliament. The Windsor, Slough and Staines Atmospheric [7] proposed two lines from Windsor. One would be to Slough to connect with the GWR main line, and one to Staines to connect with the railway from Richmond. This scheme was opposed by the GWR, the Commissioner of Woods and Forests, and Eton College. It was rejected by Parliament, whereupon:

> ". . . the astute GWR, having squared both Woods and Forests and Eton College, succeeded in getting such interests as were left to the Windsor, Slough and Staines Company transferred to them for the purpose of a Windsor branch which they had long contemplated." [8]

As a result of the duplicity of the GWR, some Windsor, Slough and Staines subscribers approached the Richmond Company, whose Directors said they were interested only if their negotiations for purchase by the LSWR broke down. The subscribers therefore went on to the LSWR, who started negotiations, the outcome of which was the formation of a new company consisting of the LSWR, Windsor Slough and Staines, and the Staines and Richmond Junction. The LSWR were to contribute capital, and work the line, with an option to purchase. In order to unify with the LSWR system the atmospheric method of traction was discarded. The company was called the Windsor, Staines and South Western (WS&SW); it was fully bought out by the LSWR in 1850.

In 1847 the company promoted a Bill containing proposals for a line from the LSWR at Richmond to Staines; a line from Staines to Windsor; a line from Staines to the LSWR main Southampton line at Pirbright; and an extension to Wokingham to join the Reading, Guildford and Reigate Railway. Except for the last, all these proposals were sanctioned though Powers lapsed for the Pirbright line and it was never built.

Again the line from Richmond was to cross the river by a bridge, but a clause in the Act provided that the line would be landscaped through the Deer Park. The Engineer was Joseph Locke, and the Contractor was the well-known Thomas Brassey who with Locke had built, amongst others, the Grand Junction, and the London and Southampton railways. Brassey agreed to have the Windsor branch ready by 31 May 1848. In fact the line from Richmond as far as Datchet was opened on 22 August 1848, after the usual Directors' Special and celebrations on 20 August. The Times reported:

> "All along the line from Richmond the residents in the villages around the stations passed appeared in large groups to welcome the passing trains, dressed in their Sunday clothing. At Twickenham, Staines, and Datchet, flags were flying . . . with music, dancing, cricket etc. . . The road is in a very good state, chiefly consisting of a gravelly bottom, and well laid. The buildings at every station, also nearly completed, are built after the same Gothic plan as those to Richmond . . . Taking the distance from Richmond to Datchet, 14 miles, a more splendid railway ride is not to be met with in England . . ." [9]

Once the independent schemes, induced by the Railway Mania of 1845-6 had collapsed, railway development settled down into a territorial struggle between the two established companies – the LSWR, with standard gauge track, and the GWR, with Brunel's Broad Gauge. This struggle was the closest that the "battle of the gauges" got to Richmond, and it was decisively won by the LSWR.

To round off the story in the upper Thames Valley, it should be recorded that the extension to Wokingham was subsequently approved and opened on 9 July 1856, giving the LSWR access to Reading via the Reading, Guildford and Reigate Railway. The link from Staines to Weybridge was completed when the Chertsey-Virginia Water section was opened on 1 October 1866. A line from Ascot to the LSWR main line at Sturt Lane Junction near Frimley was opened on 18 March 1876. Finally, the GWR reached Staines when their branch from Colnbrook opened on 2 November 1885.

Authorised also in 1847 had been a railway from Barnes to Hounslow via Brentford, which it was hoped would additionally carry excursion traffic for Kew Gardens. This scheme had been envisaged from the early days, it will be remembered, and had failed in the House of Lords when promoted by the Richmond Railway Company in August 1846. The line re-joined the Richmond-Staines railway at Feltham, and is known to this day as the Hounslow "loop". It opened to Isleworth on 22 August 1849, and to Feltham on 1 February 1850. As elsewhere in the upper Thames Valley there were no major earthworks, and the only piece of engineering construction of any significance was the crossing of the Thames at Barnes. This was done with an arched iron bridge, designed by Joseph Locke (Engineer for this line also) and J.E. Errington. It consisted of three arches of 120 feet span. Aesthetically it was, and is, unfortunate for it has defaced Barnes Terrace. The significance of the "Loop" will be shown in the next Section.

The implication of the railway having reached Staines, Windsor and then Reading, was that Richmond was no longer a terminus. From the LSWR timetable of 1859 it can be seen that the service to Reading was sparse by later standards – only five trains per day, four of which called at Richmond. The best train of the day was the 4.40pm from Waterloo Bridge (as it was initially called) which was fast to Feltham. Of five trains from Reading to Waterloo four divided at Staines into fast and slow trains, all of which called at Richmond, except for two fasts. On Sundays there were two slow trains in each direction. Horses and/or carriages could be conveyed by all trains. The service to Windsor was more generous, with twenty three "down" trains, all calling at Richmond, four of which were fast. Some trains divided at Barnes, one portion going down the 'loop' to Hounslow. There were only seventeen down trains, and sixteen up, on this line, for which the LSWR was to receive much criticism later. So far as Richmond itself was concerned, just over a decade after the line had opened, there were now twenty-three trains a day in each direction. The first up train of the morning left Richmond at 7.05, arriving at Waterloo Bridge at 7.40. A better train was the 8.41 from Richmond which reached (or was supposed to reach) Waterloo at 9.05. Only five trains a day carried third class passengers.

In the 1860s and 1870s the LSWR was much annoyed by the way middle class passengers used second class (despite the dirt and hard seats), in order to avoid the expensive first class fares. Richmond passengers also complained about the lack of trains and consequent overcrowding. According to the 1859 timetable, the fare from Waterloo to Richmond was 1s. 3d (6p) first class, 1s. 0d (5p) second class, and 9d (4p) third class (return tickets were 2s. 0d (10p) first, 1s. 6d (7 ½ p) second, third class return not being quoted for some reason. Season tickets were £16 0s yearly and £2 10d for one month first class, and second class stated to be 20% less, whilst again, third class were not quoted. There was a 10s deposit on season tickets. A working class man or woman, would not have been able to raise these sums of money and would have walked to work; the service was still intended for the middle and professional classes – the white collar commuter, the distance between their home and work becoming increasingly greater. Indeed, the LSWR attained a reputation as a 'middle class' line, which for example, is why 'Clapham' Junction was so named instead of the more topographically accurate name of 'Battersea' Junction. [12]

A final point on the 1859 timetable: it can be seen that the Sunday service was sparse. The first train left Richmond at 8.45am, reaching Waterloo at 9.30. More trains on Sundays carried third class passengers, but mid-Victorian sabbatarianism can be detected in the Sunday timetable; no trains left Waterloo between 10.45 and 1.15pm, and there was a similar gap in the up service.

With the opening of the line westwards from Richmond, changes were necessary there to cope with the new traffic; to allow more space it had been decided in March 1850 to move the engine house (shed), the turntable, and watertank to Twickenham, where land was available. Then in March 1852 tenders were invited for a new 'through' station to be sited between the bridges over Parkshot and Kew Road; this was probably opened in 1853, and lasted to 1935.

By 1864, [25] after nearly twenty years, the LSWR was providing Richmond with 24 passenger trains per day in each direction to and from Waterloo. Of the 24 down trains, 14 went on to Kingston, though there were 15 up trains from Kingston. Only two down trains provided third class accommodation, the 7.35am and the 7.10pm. There seems to have been four up trains with third

A very early photograph of the platform side of the station.

Below – the station's exterior has changed little over the years. Left shows the station with its own parcels delivery cart sometime after the line was quadrupled contrasting with the 1991 scene (right).

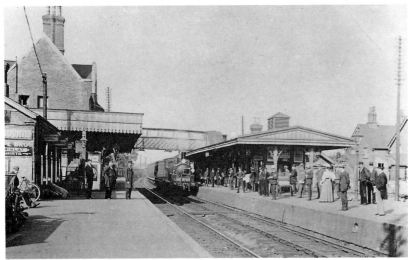

Two pictures of the old station at Twickenham at the turn of the century with (left) T1 class 0-4-4 tank No. 74 approaching with an up Windsor train.

An early twentieth century scene at Kingston showing the exterior of the original station and (right) footbridge to the through platforms with the tracks of the London United Tramways in the foreground.

class accommodation, the earliest leaving Richmond at 7.51am. The average interval between trains was about 27 minutes, the first train leaving Waterloo as late as 7.35am, the last at midnight; the first up train left Richmond at 7.01am. The loop line to Hounslow had 17 trains each way, with an average interval of 53 minutes. Each day two goods trains ran down from Nine Elms depot to Richmond, both in the early morning, one calling at Barnes. Every day a goods train left Twickenham, for Kingston at 6.30am, consisting of some of the trucks from Nine Elms, returning at 6.55pm for Nine Elms. The first up goods from Windsor had left Richmond at 4.22pm. There were also two down goods to Hounslow, but three up goods, one of which was a coal train.

KINGSTON

Unlike Richmond, Kingston (the second town of Surrey with a population of 8,147 in 1841) had no railway throughout the 1840s and 1850s. [13] Coaching interests, and a local landowner, Lord Cottenham, had prevented the London and Southampton Railway from approaching the town in the 1830s, and like some other towns without a railway, trade declined. This was in contrast to Richmond, which although well out into the country was within easy reach of London, and sought after by businessmen following in the footsteps of fashionable and leisured 18th century Londoners. By the 1850s business interests in Kingston were said to be clamouring for a railway connection.

In 1857 the GWR promoted without success a Bill for a broad-gauge branch from Southall to Richmond, with an extension to Kingston. Undeterred, another more ambitious Bill was presented in 1858, also for a line from Southall to Kingston and then to Merton, where it would join the Winbledon and Croydon railway. Another, independent Bill in the same year, the details of which are obscure, was from what was described as "North London", to Paddington, Richmond, Hampton Court, and Kingston. The LSWR defeated these schemes by offering to construct reverse curves at Kew and Barnes (more of which later), and a Twickenham to Hampton Wick branch, terminating at the western end of Kingston Bridge. This was authorised in 1859 and although there was local opposition Kingston business interests succeeded in getting the line extended across the river to a terminus at the Richmond Road. Accounts vary as to whether the LSWR welcomed this development; they were certainly irritated at still having to build a station at Hampton Wick as well as in Kingston. The line opened on 1 July 1863, the only other intermediate station being Teddington. The main engineering work on an otherwise flat and simple formation was the bridge at Kingston; this was designed by J.E. Errington and was of five cast iron arches. The opening of the line enabled travellers from Richmond to reach Southampton, the Isle of Wight, Salisbury and the south-west without travelling to Waterloo (they would have just had the short omnibus journey on to Surbiton).

As always, the fares were considered high – 9d (4p) to Richmond in comparison to 6d (2 ½ p) by bus, for example. [14] But:-

> "The new line to Kingston seems to be doing a deal of business, principally from the North London districts. If it is wished to obtain the local traffic between Richmond, Hampton Court, and Teddington, the fares must not be kept at their present excessive amount. We can get better accommodation at less expense by the Omnibus. It is essentially a pleasure traffic, and only to be developed by making the fares as low as possible." [15]

And as the novelty began to wear off, Kingston people began to tire of the 'roundabout' route, as it became known (and still is) to London, even if the North London Railway (NLR), trains now extended to Kingston from Richmond were well patronised. Also in April 1866 the LSWR started a new service to the City. Seven trains per day were routed as follows: Kingston-Richmond-Clapham Junction, then crossing under the LSWR main line, and then eastwards to Wandsworth Road over the London, Chatham and Dover Company lines (LCDR), then Brixton to Loughborough Road, then north to Camberwell-Elephant and Castle-Blackfriars-Ludgate Hill. [16]

In 1868 services were introduced of ten trains per day from Kensington to Ludgate Hill, one train to Twickenham, five to Kingston, and four to Clapham Junction only. These services were the precursors of the services via Kensington, opened a year later (see next section).

In 1866 an independent Bill was promoted for a City, Kingston and Richmond railway, which would have to run through Wimbledon and Petersham. This was "plunging deep into LSWR territory", [17] and was backed by the South Eastern Railway (SER), but was eventually withdrawn, probably through lack of capital. Various schemes were mooted for lines from the east, which persuaded the LSWR to obtain powers for a line through Norbiton and Malden to join the main line at Wimbledon. This opened on 1 January 1869, with a service of eleven trains a day to Ludgate Hill, via the Tooting, Merton and Wimbledon Railway. Passengers for Waterloo changed at Wimbledon. The North London services once again terminated at Richmond, LSWR and North London engines being changed at Kew.

Over the years the pattern of services at Kingston changed so that the principal service became the "roundabout": Waterloo-Wimbledon-Kingston-Richmond-Waterloo, and vice-versa. The service to Ludgate Hill withered away.

The railway from Twickenham to Kingston was a major stimulation to middle-class housing development from 1863 onwards, especially at Teddington and Strawberry Hill. Back in 1852 the "Builder" reported that the LSWR (like other railway companies) offered season tickets to builders who would then give them to occupiers in the vicinity of the line. [18]

A writer in the 1880s said of Teddington:

> ". . . a few years ago – long since the accession of Queen Victoria – Teddington was a quiet rural village . . . Now all is changed: rows of spruce villas and 'neat' terraces have sprung up along the roads to Twickenham and Hampton Wick, and all over the upper end of the village, which must now soon call itself a town, with its grand 'hotels' and magnificent 'stores' which have fairly driven out the keepers of its hostelries, and threaten to swallow up the 'small trader' class. This growth of Teddington is in great measure owing to the introduction of the railway" [19]

From 1861 to 1871 the population of Teddington had nearly quadrupled – from 1,183 to 4,063. Of Strawberry Hill he was pessimistic:

> "Though Strawberry Hill still stands, and though its grounds are as yet intact, yet probably they are both doomed to destruction. 'Coming events' they say, 'cast their shadows before them'; and therefore it may be worth while to add that on the opposite side of the road a large tract of land, extending up to the Strawberry Hill railway station has been taken in hand by a firm of London builders, who are rapidly covering the green fields with villas." [20]

But of Twickenham, this writer was more sanguine:

> "Although the village and its surroundings have lost much of their rural seclusion of late years by the formation of a railway through its very centre, and the rapid increase of modern dwelling-houses in all directions, much of its sylvan beauties are still visible, and its riverside aspect is as attractive as of old." [21]

The landowning and property development interests had had to persuade the LSWR to open a station at Strawberry Hill, and had offered to pay one third of the cost. As Mr Jackson says: "A vaguely Italianate two platform station distinguished with some delicate-looking ironwork under its canopies was the result". [22] This station opened in 1873 and was enlarged in 1935; the original station house survives, of typical LSWR design, similar to Gillingham (Dorset) and others west of Salisbury built a decade earlier. Teddington also has its original station house with the 'Railway Hotel' next door, with a saloon bar full of railwayana.

Strawberry Hill station was situated to the north of the junction with the Shepperton branch, which had opened in 1864 (see below). A further operational development was the opening of a flyover on 22 October 1883 carrying the up Kingston line over the Windsor lines into a new platform at the north side of Twickenham station. This was extended to form an additional up line to St Margarets on 26 November 1899.

THE SHEPPERTON LINE

Originally part of the scheme to link Chertsey with London, this line was called the "Thames Valley

Line" for many years, and was eventually integrated into the LSWR system. It never reached Chertsey, instead it ended in a potato field outside Shepperton village, "as if weary of going further". [23] The original scheme had been to link with the GWR, and so the Thames Valley Railway was no more than sufficient to keep that company out of what the LSWR regarded as its territory, i.e. it was a blocking line (more of this problem later). As can be seen to this day, Shepperton was designed as a through station.

A contemporary account welcomed the opening of the line in November 1864:

> ". . . the New Line to Shepperton, Sunbury etc . . . must be of advantage to Richmond, which is now the 'Metropolis' of a much larger area than in Walpole's time. There is a large and wealthy class of inhabitants in the Sunbury District, who will not fail to use the railway to visit Richmond and become customers at its shops. It is true that equal facilities are offered for London; but a good town like Richmond will, we venture to say, intercept the best part of the custom . . ." [24]

The service was sparse – just seven trains each way on weekdays, via Richmond, taking 50 minutes to Waterloo. There were therefore long gaps between trains, which were even longer on Sundays as there were only four trains on that day. Third class passengers were only carried on the first train of the day, each way.

By 1866 the service had been improved slightly as there were now ten trains each way. Twenty years later this had increased to sixteen, but ten of them involved changing at Twickenham or Strawberry Hill. In 1915 – just before electrification – there were twenty-three trains, but the fastest still took 48 minutes. Most trains ran via Richmond, some combining with Kingston or Windsor trains at Twickenham. Goods services started with one train per day; by 1909 this had increased to two. The line served only small communities, but was given greater importance in 1878, when Kempton Park racecourse was opened. To facilitate traffic, Fulwell curve, ½ mile south of Strawberry Hill, was brought into use in 1894, allowing traffic via Kingston, but at first only one regular passenger service was routed via Kingston. Inside the triangle thus created, a locomotive depot was built in 1897 replacing the small engine sheds at Twickenham and Kingston. It accommodated fifty locomotives and employed 500 men, but in 1922 was superseded by Feltham depot. From 1916 Strawberry Hill has been used as an electric train depot, the "roundabout" and Shepperton branch being electrified in that year.

In the last quarter of the 19th century discontent about the train services built up; in 1885 Hampton ratepayers campaigned for an extension of the District line from Hounslow (which it had reached in 1883) to Hampton. In 1893 the local Boards of Sunbury, Teddington, and Hampton tried to persuade the LSWR to extend the line from Shepperton to Chertsey, but the company refused because of the cost of a bridge over the Thames.

THE RAILWAY AT RICHMOND IN THE 1860s

> "Enginemen in charge of Trains on the Loop, Richmond and Windsor Lines, must approach the Junctions at Kew and Barnes, and also the Twickenham and Richmond Stations, with great caution, and at such a rate of speed that their Trains can be quickly stopped if necessary." [26]

Having traced these developments west of Richmond, we can now give some consideration to the transport scene two decades after the railway from London had first opened. In railway history generally, 1870 is taken as a turning point; the end of the heroic, but primitive railway, and the beginning of a technically more advanced system, with bigger carriages, bigger locomotives, smoother track, and mechanical signalling.

Although regular steamboat services to Richmond died out in the 1850s, it is important to remember that even if the railway had revolutionised travel, other modes of conveyance, for example horse drawn waggons and horse buses, grew in order to 'feed' the railway.

From Richmond a horse-bus owned by the Richmond Conveyance Company ran to London, with whom the journey took 1½ hours, as it had done in the 1830s. There was also a horse-bus between

Richmond and Surbiton station. These services probably lasted until the advent of the motor bus – because they met the demand for short, intermediate journeys. More significantly, horse-drawn transport would have been needed to distribute coal and goods from Richmond station, as well as the heavy, bulk materials arriving by river barge – a mode which survived into the twentieth century. The overall effect of the railway was viewed at the time as beneficial:-

> ". . . since the railway was made, property in Richmond has doubled in value, the houses nearly doubled in number, and we really believe, tradesmen's profits have doubled in amount." [27]

Although part of this was attributable to the railway, it must also have been caused by the overall population growth.

But attitudes to the LSWR and the services it actually provided were different. There was resentment about the company's monopoly position in the provision of railway travel, and proposals by the NLR in 1863 to build a terminus at the western foot of Richmond Hill were welcomed. In fact this scheme was dropped in 1866, but by this time the town's population had increased to 22,781, and it was felt the LSWR could not cope with the demand for railway services. A railway to Richmond was being proposed from Acton and it was very much hoped in Richmond that it would be built by one of the contending companies other than the LSWR. It was not – Parliament gave powers to the LSWR and there was much anger in Richmond about this (not an uncommon situation; the business community of Southampton detested the LSWR, and encouraged, unsuccessfully, the GWR to reach the town). Hiscoke complained about the LSWR's anxiety to preserve its monopoly of the profitable "pleasure traffic" (which was the bulk of the traffic) to and from the town. The commuter traffic to London was a thing of the future. Hiscoke said that the LSWR had:-

> ". . . proverbially no feeling. What we contend for is this, that Richmond has much need of better railway accommodation – that she has a right to share in the facilities which the new lines opening in and around London give . . ." [28]

There was also continuing resentment about the LSWR's fares. One sentence in an article in 1864 expressed this view:-

> "Railways have existed sufficiently long to convince their Directors that cheap fares especially in pleasure traffic, pay much better than dear ones; yet this truth is not recognised between Richmond and Windsor, and is altogether disregarded between Richmond and Kingston." [29]

– though one has to assume that the Directors knew their business; they presumably set fares at the highest level the market would bear, even though this was anti-social.

Another complaint with the LSWR was over Waterloo Station "now becoming the worst station in the land" according to Hiscoke. [30] The facilities had not kept pace with the expansion in LSWR services and it had become over-crowded and chaotic. It had opened in 1848, it will be remembered, "decidedly on the simple side" as one writer has put it. [31] It was built on arches with approach ramps on either side of the platforms, and grew piecemeal; the "Windsor" station was added in 1862, the "south" or "Cyprus" station was added in 1878, and the "north" or "Khartoum" station added in 1885 (this is where platforms 16 to 21 were until 1990). By the turn of the century the muddle had become impossible even for the staff let along bewildered passengers. For a hilarious description of Waterloo see Jerome K. Jerome's "Three Men in a Boat". From another source we are told that the booking office was about 535 yards from the main line departure platform, No. 1, so it was suggested that "elderly passengers should have themselves labelled as luggage and pushed in a barrow to the train". [32]

A complete rebuilding was started in 1902 but was delayed by the First World War, and the present station was opened in 1922 – the last year of the LSWR. To continue this digression, there had been four tracks from Vauxhall, from 1848, which were widened to six in 1892, and to eight in 1916. The first signal box, a 47 lever installation, was opened in 1867; this developed into the well-known 'A' box of 1892, to be replaced by a new box operating colour light signals in 1936 itself superseded in 1990.

One of the other principal complaints about Waterloo was the distance from the City – a problem

Several of Beattie's 0-6-0's ended their days on local freight workings. Left is double framed No. 286-A and (below) an unidentifiable single framed example.

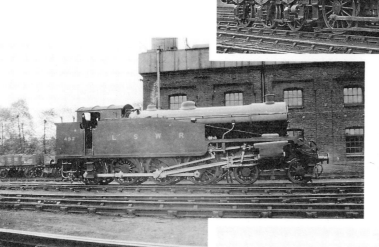

Four G16 4-8-0 tank engines were built in 1918 for shunting at Feltham Marshalling Yard and they were shedded at Strawberry Hill until Feltham shed was ready.

The present scene with class 455 unit No. 916 and Traction Test Unit No. 053 (formerly 2 EPB No. 6291)

which the LSWR had always hoped to remedy by building its own City terminus. In the event, the LSWR did reach the City, by their own tube railway – the second in London – opened in 1898, now known as the Waterloo and City line, or pejoratively as the "Drain".

Charing Cross and Cannon Street stations had been opened in 1864 and 1866 respectively at enormous cost, but the SER, and people at Richmond wanted to be able to get to these stations. The best the LSWR could offer was a new service from Richmond to Clapham Junction, then over the LCDR lines to Ludgate Hill. It was suggested that as passengers wanted to go to Cannon Street a connecting curve should be put in at Waterloo to permit through running. [33] Another question was:

> "Are we ever to be taken into the Charing Cross Station the most central one
> in London and the one that to the ladies, no inconsiderable part of Richmond traf-
> fic, is the most accommodating? Twice a year, perhaps, some ladies, principally
> elder ones, may wish to go into the City; but every week and every day, some,
> both old and young, wish to indulge in a walk through Regent Street and the
> other thoroughfares of the West End." [34]

Six months later, when the curve through Waterloo was opened:

> "We wish we could see in it a hope that the Richmond Traffic would also be
> enabled to obtain access to Charing Cross and London Bridge, and, ultimately, to
> Cannon Street. But we fear that we are doomed to disappointment." [35]

A further suggestion was that passengers should be able to get out at the 'ticket-taking' stop at Westminster Road in order to get to Westminster. [36] Hiscoke finally said:-

> "as the South Western authorities when they have the choice of means seem
> inclined to take the worse (instead of which they could render a great service to
> a very important and hitherto very patient body of their customers)." [37]

It was said that the LSWR was often called "The London Slow and Weary", [38] and an elderly gentleman, reminiscing to a local newspaper about the slowness of trains in the 19th century told two anecdotes:

> "A man's dog followed him to the station, but he drove it off: he was surprised to
> find it waiting for him at the next station."

> "I have seen a print . . . representing a coster-monger in his donkey-barrow
> drawing an engine and train after him with the passengers leaning out of the
> windows waving their hats and cheering at the pace they were going." [39]

An improvement was the opening, after delays, of Clapham Junction in 1863, so that " . . . day trips to Brighton for the sea breeze now became popular", [40] but two years later disenchantment had set in:

> ". . . all trains ought to stop at Clapham Junction. It is a place of almost uni-
> versal exchange, and it is too bad to make persons go into London, and thence
> take cabs to Victoria or elsewhere, to get to any of the numberless places which
> may be reached by trains passing Clapham Junction." [41]

Later in the year, 1865, Hiscoke had more to say about Clapham Junction:-

> "The Directors of the various lines using Clapham Junction seem in a conspir-
> acy to make it as little useful as possible. To utilise properly every train ought to
> stop there: it is calculated for an almost universal exchange; yet for the sake of a
> few paltry pence, passengers are taken on to the various termini, inflicting not
> only delay but heavy cab expense on the unhappy passenger. At present also the
> few South Western trains, which travel at intervals, might as well be given up;
> an arrangement with the Brighton company to take the South Western traffic on
> would answer every purpose and ensure more frequent opportunities of getting
> to Kensington." [42]

Once the novelty of railway travel wore off, and by the mid-century it certainly had, passengers realised that carriage accommodation left a lot to be desired. At Richmond there was much criticism of LSWR on this issue; an American visitor said at the time:

> "The first class is luxurious, light and splendid with plate glass sides and fur-

nished with capacious spring seats and with every accommodation for the bestowing of bundles, hats, and umbrellas. The second class carriages form a lamentable contrast to this: it is as hard, bare, and uncomely a box as oak boards can make it; its seats are uncushioned and frequently dirtied by the boots and baskets of railway and market men. There seems to be little or no distinction between the second and third class carriages, excepting in this, that the second class carriages are resorted to by the most respectable people on account of the expensiveness of the first." [43]

The railway was still patronised mainly by the upper and middle classes; the vast majority of workmen walked to work, and over greater distances than would be acceptable today. Nevertheless the trains were still overcrowded, and by 1865 the LSWR had increased the number in each direction at Richmond to thirty-three. It was reported in February 1865 that:-

"recently nearly fifty persons having first class tickets were compelled to go by second class carriages or stay behind." [44]

On the Hounslow loop the service was considered to be even worse, with only half the number of trains that served Richmond. A public meeting had been called in Brentford in the Spring of 1865 chaired by a Colonel Murray. The number of trains to and from Richmond, daily, 61, had been contrasted with the 36 on the loop line. It was stated at the meeting that the population of Richmond, Twickenham and Mortlake was 22,781, whereas that of Chiswick, Kew, Isleworth, Hounslow and Brentford was 31,322. But as Hiscoke pointed out there are more visitors from London to Richmond than to Brentford, therefore:

". . . the discrepancy between the two lines ceases to be so glaring. A Committee was appointed to confer with the Directors, and we wish them success, for in truth more trains are wanted on both lines. At Richmond it is often difficult to procure a place, and extra carriages are not kept there to meet the want". [45]

To the end of the century and up to electrification of the line complaints from Hounslow and Brentford were loud and frequent. A fairly strongly worded editorial in the Richmond and Twickenham Times on 25 November 1876, following correspondence in the paper, said:

"The management of the loop line . . . has long been notorious for the most deficient service, the vilest station accommodation, and the most defective arrangements to be found on any railway in England (had the Editor visited all of them?) The natural outcome of all this has been a proportionate depreciation in the value of house property, a depression of trade . . ."

There had recently been a public meeting in Hounslow to protest to the Directors of the LSWR. A committee and deputation had been formed. Comparison was made with Twickenham, only two miles away and having what was regarded as a good service; also the now familiar complaint was made about Waterloo station not being centrally situated and being a muddle. But the protest had some effect, as later protests were to, and the LSWR provided an extra train per day. The Feltham curve, enabling trains to run direct from Hounslow to Twickenham was opened without Parliamentary authority on 1 January 1883.

Notes and References

1.   Timetables of the London and South Western Railway, November 1859.
2.   R.A. Williams, The London and South Western Railway, vol. 1, 1968, p.168.
3.   Report from the Board of Trade, op.cit.
4.   The Railway mania and its Aftermath, H.G. Lewin, 1936 (repr. 1968), p.139.
5.   Lewin, op.cit., p.140.
6.   Lewin, op.cit., p.141.
7.   A method of traction whereby carriages are drawn by a vacuum maintained in a pipe between the rails.
8.   Lewin, op.cit., p.141.
9.   The Times, 28 August 1848.

10. Williams, op.cit., p.172.
11. Lewin, op.cit., p.300.
12. T. Sherwood, Why Clapham Junction?, Railway Magazine, August 1986.
13. The present Surbiton Station was called Kingston-on-Railway even though it is over a mile from the town.
14. A.A. Jackson, London's Local Railways, 1978, p.57.
15. Hiscoke, op.cit., no.6, August 1863, p.6.
16. See map, owned by the LCDR, this station was closed in 1929.
17. Williams, op.cit., vol. 2, 1973, p.14.
18. The Builder, vol. 10, 1852, p.253.
19. E. Walford, Greater London. vol. 1, undated, p.123.
20, 21. Ibid.
22. Jackson, op.cit., p.58.
23. The Rev. W.J. Scott, quoted in Jackson, op.cit., p.65.
24. Hiscoke, op.cit., no.21, November 1864, p.2.
25. The information in this paragraph is from the LSWR working timetable of December 1864, copy in Twickenham Local History Library. A working timetable is for railway staff and shows all train movements, including goods and light engines.
26. Ibid.
27. Hiscoke, op.cit., no.13, March 1864, p.3.
28. Hiscoke, op.cit., no.11, January 1864, p.3.
29. Hiscoke, op.cit., no.21, November 1864, p.2.
30. Hiscoke, op.cit., no.11, January 1864, p.2.
31. E. Course, London Railways, 1962, p.84.
32. Reminiscences of John Eustace Anderson, Richmond Herald, 11.1.1908.
33. The SER put in a curve as required by their Act, in 1864. It ran through the concourse of Waterloo Station and faced London Bridge. There was a short-lived service from Kensington to London Bridge, and from 1875 seven trains per day ran from Willesden Junction to London Bridge. The curve was closed in 1911. Waterloo East Station had been opened by the SER as Waterloo Junction in 1869.
34. Hiscoke, op.cit., no.22, December 1864, pp.1-2. A curve facing Charing Cross was never put in.
35. Hiscoke, op.cit., no.28, June 1865, p.65.
36. Collecting tickets outside termini was general practice until ticket barriers were introduced in the 1870s.
37. Hiscoke, op.cit., no.22, December 1864, p.2.
38. M. Nemet, RTT, 27 February 1960.
39. John Eustace Anderson, op.cit.
40. Richmond and Twickenham Times, 27 February 1960.
41. Hiscoke, op.cit., no.24, February 1865, p.14.
42. Hiscoke, op.cit., no.28, June 1865, p.65.
43. RTT 27 February 1960.
44. Hiscoke, op.cit., no.24, February 1865, p.14.
45. Ibid.

Part III
Railways from north of the Thames

"Few places have suffered as much from the changes which the whirligig of time brings with it, as the once charming village of Richmond.". [1]

Turning now to the railway schemes from this direction, of which mention was made in the previous chapter, the earliest proposal was from a nominally independent company, the North and South Western Junction (NSWJR) with which Chadwick of the Richmond Railway Company was involved. This was in about 1847, and the line was to run seven miles from Harrow on the London and North Western Railway (LNWR), to Brentford on the LSWR loop line. The idea was not to serve Richmond, but to provide a strategic and profitable north-south link for goods, especially coal (a scheme linking Manchester to Southampton for this purpose had failed in the previous year, 1846). This was an alternative. At a time when many big towns still had no railway, this proposal was greeted with ridicule (but so were many others and in spirit this line survived), and opposed by both the LSWR and the GWR. The Bill was rejected by the House of Lords in 1848, Chadwick having been "roughly handled", [2] under cross-examination. As another writer has said: "such a proposition required a great deal of careful political footwork to bring it to life". [3]

A modified proposal appeared in 1850, once again for goods, with no mention of passenger services, for a three and a half mile line from the LNWR at what was to become Willesden Junction to Brentford, this time supported by the LNWR and LSWR, but opposed by the GWR who contended that goods could be carried from Manchester to Southampton on their system, via Oxford. At the Parliamentary Committee stage of the Manchester-Southampton Bill in 1846 the GWR had undertaken to provide a mixed-gauge line from Oxford to Basingstoke, but by 1851 had still not done so (it was still Broad Gauge). The provisional Board of the NSWJR consisted of LSWR and LNWR directors who were most anxious to keep a competitor out, especially the GWR with the complications of the Broad Gauge, and they explained to the House of Lords Committee that goods traffic from the north came to the LNWR goods yard at Camden and was then carted across London to the LSWR at Nine Elms. For this reason, presumably, the junction at Willesden faced Camden, and not north-west, and this unintentionally enabled passenger services to run to Richmond, as will be explained shortly.

The NSWJR was incorporated in July 1851, and after various delays opened for goods traffic on 15 February 1853, and for passengers on 1 August of that year. Four trains per day were provided by the North London Railway from Camden Town to Kew Junction, where a rudimentary station was constructed. This was to become known as 'Old' Kew station. There were connections on the NLR with Fenchurch Street, and for five months in 1854 trains ran on to Windsor. From 20 May 1858 trains ran on to Richmond and Twickenham by reversing onto the 'Loop' line at Kew, proceeding to Barnes and then reversing again on to the Richmond line.

To eliminate this 'Z' shaped route both the NSWJR and LSWR promoted direct routes from Kew, but the LNWR for some reason opposed them and the schemes were dropped in the 1854 session. In 1857 the House of Lords rejected an independently promoted extension from Kew to Richmond, and in the following year also rejected a broad gauge extension from the GWR at Brentford Dock. Presumably the LSWR had opposed the former scheme; they had certainly opposed the latter, and it was to counter these proposals that the LSWR had put on through trains to Twickenham in 1858. LSWR carriages ran to Hampstead by alternate trains and from Willesden Junction to Camden Road via Hampstead Heath. Some carriages even worked through to Fenchurch Street. These trains

A pre-grouping scene looking north with a LNWR parcels train. The Richmond line diverged at the north end of the station.

A local train for Clapham Junction stands in one of the bay platforms in early Southern Railway days with 0-4-2 tank No. B629 and carriages of London, Brighton and South Coast Railway origin.

LMS electric train on the Willesden Junction – Earls Court service.

Post-war view of a District line E stock train on the exhibition shuttle service to Earls Court.

took 90 minutes to get from Richmond to Fenchurch Street (10 minutes more from Twickenham). Whether this would have been a quicker journey to the City than going via Waterloo and then by horse-bus, is doubtful.

The carriages at this time were still four-wheelers, with rudimentary springs, and no heating. Steam heating was not introduced generally until 1884, but on these trains gas was used for heating towards the end of the century. The lighting was primitive; in December 1862 the LSWR rejected a request from the North London to fit their carriages with gas lighting – so they continued with oil lamps. Rape oil was used and the lamps were inserted through the roof on the carriage. To supplement this, regular passengers and commuters had their own candles, in holders, with spring which kept the flame steady. The North London, after introducing gas lighting in 1862, were followed by the Metropolitan and District, who used it from their inception.

The NSWJR came under NLR management about 1860, with the latter company continuing to provide the passenger services. In 1871 it was leased to the LNWR, Midland, and NLR; the NLR still continued to provide services, but the NSWJR retained its identity down to the amalgamations of 1923.

In 1858 two more Bills were presented: it will be remembered that one was for a line from the GWR at Southall to Merton, via Isleworth, Kingston and Malden. The other, details of which are obscure, was from what was described as "North London", to Paddington, Richmond, Hampton Court, and Kingston. As already noted the LSWR defeated these schemes to reach Kingston by offering to construct reverse curves at Kew and Barnes, and by constructing a Twickenham to Hampton Wick branch. These proposals were authorised in August 1859, but the LSWR delayed work on the curves – having defeated the other schemes they saw no need to hurry – and the new lines were not ready until 1 February 1862. The two junctions on the curve at Barnes were known as Chiswick Junction and Mortlake Junction. Surprisingly, there was still no improvement in the timetable. [4] Trains were extended to Kingston on 1 July 1863.

In 1866 the LSWR obtained Powers to build a curve, from the GWR branch at Brentford Dock, south eastwards down to the Hounslow loop. This would have let GWR trains from the main line at Southall run over LSWR metals to Richmond, and given the town direct access to the Midlands and the West Country. Construction was prevented by shortage of money.

THE KENSINGTON AND RICHMOND LINE

Fearing that an independently promoted line would attempt to fill the vacuum, the NSWJR proposed a connecting line from their Hammersmith and Chiswick branch to the proposed Hammersmith and City (H & C) line at Shepherd's Bush (see map). They were persuaded to withdraw this scheme by the LSWR, who had plans of their own. The early 1860s saw what historians have called the third railway 'mania' (this one also being called the metropolitan mania), when there was a flood of proposals for 'outer circle' lines around London (at this time the western edge of London was at Earl's Court). This activity had been stimulated by the success of the first underground railway, from Bishops Road (Paddington) to Farringdon, in 1863, and also by the House of Lords Select Committee Report on railways around London.

Two schemes that concern us were the Barnes, Hammersmith and Kensington, and the Kensington and North and South London Junction. Both were rejected by the Lords in 1863, after strong opposition by the LSWR and the West London Railway.

In addition to the NSWJR scheme previously mentioned, there was a proposal from the H & C to extend their mixed gauge line through Turnham Green to Kew and then south to Richmond, and possibly to Petersham, their aim being to link Richmond with north London. This company was owned by the GWR and the Metropolitan, and their line opened on 13th June 1864 had been conceived as a westerly extension of the Farringdon-Paddington line.

From Westbourne Grove to Hammersmith it ran through open country, mainly market gardens, circumventing the built-up area, but the line was built on a viaduct in order not to impede housing development. The generous width of the viaduct is evidence of the Broad Gauge. From its opening there was a half-hourly service of broad gauge trains from Farringdon to Hammersmith but in the following year standard gauge track was laid, and according to some sources, [5] the broad gauge was lifted west of Latimer Road as early as March 1869. The line was carried over the West London Railway, and there was a broad gauge spur down to Kensington. This was destroyed by bombing in 1940 and later removed, but the stub of the viaduct is still visible west of Latimer Road station.

It should be noted here that from the beginning of the railway age, the companies attempted to carve out territories in which they could maintain monopoly positions (thus defeating the logic of free enterprise). But there had always been areas where the territories overlapped. By virtue of the success of the 1846 railway from Nine Elms, and by virtue of Richmond being "one of the chief river-side towns and . . . already becoming a high class dormitory suburb, from which the prosperous commuters were finding the journey on to the City from Waterloo tedious" [6] Richmond, as well as Hammersmith, had become a pressure point to the west of London, and so the LSWR were anxious to keep other companies out. As they were already running trains up the West London line to Kensington, their solution was to propose a line from that station to Hammersmith, via Shepherd's Bush, and then along the same route as the H & C had proposed to Richmond. As one writer has put it: "It sounds a roundabout way of getting from Richmond or Hammersmith to the City, but it was done . . ." [7] But the LSWR must have chosen the Shepherds Bush route in order to keep Kensington, with its middle class traffic.

When the three Bills were presented to Parliament, the House of Commons Select Committee sensibly decided to hear all three together. The LSWR Bill was heard first, in March 1864, and in addition to being opposed by the other railway companies, including the LNWR, was also opposed by the Metropolitan Board of Works (who opposed many railway schemes because they affected their roads), the Grand Junction Water Company, and Richmond Vestry (it is not certain why, but it may have been the antipathy to this Company). As normally happened, various individuals affected by the scheme petitioned against it. In their evidence, the LSWR made the most of the fact that they already had a station at Richmond. They gave an assurance that they would enlarge their station, pointing out that the H & C would need a separate station. The LNWR started making difficulties over the junction at Kensington and congestion at Kensington Station which only had one platform; as principal shareholder of the NLR, they wanted to continue running through the existing LSWR station, at Richmond, on to Kingston, and not into a new terminus.

The other Bills failed, including the H & C, lamented by Hiscoke:

> "So far as Richmond is concerned, the Parliamentary campaign is over . . . the 'Metropolitan and Richmond', has, we regret to say, been lost on Standing Orders . . . and an active opponent (active enough in opposition – slow enough in self improvement) has taken advantage of this, and succeeded in defeating the Bill for this session." [8]

Provision was made in the LSWR Act for the extension of the broad gauge from Hammersmith to Richmond, the cost to be borne by the GWR. Though this was never carried out it can be seen that the Parliamentary process had produced a compromise. There was also to be a connection from the NSWJR at Acton Junction, south to join the Kensington and Richmond (K & R) at what is now Gunnersbury junction. Over this the NLR would have running powers to Richmond and on to Kingston via a connection to the LSWR 'old' line, east of Richmond station. Later, in 1878 there was an eastwards curve from Bollo Lane Junction to Acton Lane Junctions, completing what has been known as the Gunnersbury triangle, the northern side of which was closed in 1965 when coal trains to West Kensington were withdrawn. Before crossing the Thames, the line crossed over the Hounslow loop, and a westerly curve was provided down to it, enabling trains from Hammersmith to run to Hounslow.

The H & C were concerned about the disruption the LSWR line would cause in crossing their line north of Hammersmith, and so strained were relations between the two companies that a further Act was passed in 1865 giving the LSWR more time to sort out the muddle. It also saved them about £50,000 on works, and provided for a separate line from Kensington which passed under the H & C, connection being made further south by a spur from the H & C to the LSWR. This enabled Metropolitan and GWR trains to run on to Richmond.

In giving evidence to the House of Lords Committee, Archibald Scott, General Manager of the LSWR, said:

> "In my experience I have not known a line which had so many objections taken to it, and what I may call objections particularly applicable to junctions and stations."

He was referring to Kensington and to Hammersmith, where there was to be a joint station, but by yet more legislation in 1867 this was abandoned and the H & C station was moved further south to its present position on the Broadway, opening on 1 December 1868. The LSWR station, called Grove Road, was built close by on the embankment; because of this it had wooden platforms which were "sheltered by generous canopies supported on decorated cast-iron columns. At street level on the east side was a plain two-storey station house with round-arched windows". [9] A contemporary description was that it was "handsome and commodious". [10] It was at the point where the line changed direction from south to west, and so the platforms were curved. In compliance with the Act, the LSWR provided a covered footway from Grove Road to the H & C terminus. This station, rebuilt in 1908 by the GWR, still bares evidence of its history with its unmistakeable Great Western footbridge at the end of the platforms.

The LSWR line continued west on a viaduct for just over a mile. This viaduct is twenty feet high with arches of twenty foot span, and was probably built in order not to block roads and impede housing development. Later the pioneer Bedford Park middle class garden city development was started, which Turnham Green station at the western end of the viaduct was able to serve. Bedford Park depended on the railway taking its residents to central London and the City, and the relationship between this model housing estate (1875-8) and the railway is worthy of further study. The LSWR may have offered cheap season tickets.

The line continued in a shallow cutting to Gunnersbury Junction, the station there being called Brentford Road until it was changed to Gunnersbury in 1871. As already noted, the line crossed the Hounslow loop, and then crossed the Thames on a five-span wrought-iron lattice girder bridge, decorated with gothic capitals on its red brick abutments. As Mr Jackson says, the bridge "successfully disfigures the attractive riverside hamlet of Strand-on-the-Green". [11] Kew Gardens station, a requirement of the 1864 Act, consisted of a two storey- house of yellow brick, "with nicely detailed round-headed openings". [12] Slightly to the west is a pavilion, containing a bar, an unusual feature for a small station. Another feature of this line was that "block" signalling (superseding "time-interval" signalling) was installed attracting considerable attention in the railway world. The line was among the earliest to have diagrams of signalling issued to Inspectors, Drivers, Guards, Signalmen, Pointsmen and Porters. These instructions had day and night codes for engine head signals, whistle codes, and the general instructions filled 27 foolscap sheets. [13]

Meanwhile it should be noted that a station had been opened at Willesden Junction in 1866, used by NLR passengers to and from Richmond; this station was chaotic until reconstructed, and was nicknamed "Bewildering Junction". Also, at this time a second platform was provided at Kensington. The line from Hammersmith to Richmond was constructed by the well-known contractors Brassey and Ogilvy by the end of 1868 and was opened for services on 1 January 1869. Unsurprisingly the immediate reaction, voiced by the West London Observer, was that fares were too high, and as before, the LSWR were forced to reduce them to a reasonable level. Resentment and discontent with the level of LSWR fares rumbled on to the end of the century. For example, in 1895 a body called the "Railway Accommodation Committee" sent a long memorandum to the LSWR complaining about the level of fares charged to Richmond in comparison to other lines. They also complained about the lack of facilities such as cheap day returns etc. According to them the return fare from Waterloo to Barnes was 8d, whereas the single fare from Waterloo to Richmond was 9d.

An hourly service was provided from Richmond to Waterloo via Kensington which took 47 minutes, about which the West London Observer said:

> ". . . in point of quickness and comfort this new railway is to be found more agreeable than the underground line (the H & C)."

In fact the LSWR services were advertised as the "over-ground" route, and although the H & C "underground" gave:

> "Real accommodation in the shape of roomy and illuminated carriages and low
> fares",

it had other drawbacks:

> "Itinerant musicians are again(?) permitted to do their screeching, and dried
> fish and large baskets of vegetables are permitted to be placed in your lap". [14]

The LSWR ran ten trains per day to Ludgate Hill (these came off the West London line at Longhedge Junction, Battersea, and ran via Herne Hill). In fact this was an extension of the Ludgate Hill-Kensington service, and was the LSWR's bid to get from Richmond into the City of London. The 14 ½ mile journey took 65 minutes and has been described by one writer as follows:

> ". . . as the trains wended their way . . . and changed direction from south-east
> to north-east, south-east again and then east and north, it must have seemed
> desperately roundabout compared with a horse-bus from Hammersmith to
> Piccadilly" [15]

or, as someone else has put it, the journey was:

> "guaranteed to cure the most obstinate case of insomnia". [16]

This replaced the service from Kingston and Richmond via Barnes and Clapham Junction to Ludgate Hill, started in 1866. It will be remembered that a Kingston-Ludgate Hill via Norbiton and Wimbledon service started at this time. Also on 1 January 1869, NLR trains, which had been running from Broad Street since it opened in 1865 (services from Fenchurch Street having ceased in 1868), used the new direct route from Acton Junction to Richmond.

As already noted, a terminus station had been provided at Richmond, on the north east side of the existing site, for the reception of these new services. The station at Richmond now consisted of three elements: the original terminus of 1846, now relegated to coal and goods, the fate of many obsolete stations; the through Windsor/Kingston/Shepperton station of 1853; and the terminus, known as the "new" station. This had three platform faces when it opened; an additional platform, with two faces, was added after the arrival of the District Railway, around 1877. At the time of opening, the "new" station was used by the LSWR and NLR – other companies came later. Separate offices in the two stations were maintained, the NSWJR maintaining their own booking office and clerks until 1917. [17] With the advent of direct services the curves at Kew and Barnes were no longer needed for passenger services. The former continued to be used for goods services and is still in place, occasionally used also for excursion trains; the latter was removed in 1881. Its path can still be discerned from the alignment of 'railway side' cottages, and the stub of the embankment at the south west end of Barnes Bridge station.

On 1 June 1870 the GWR exercised the running powers granted to them by the K & R Act, and started a service at intervals of approximately one hour from Paddington to Hammersmith on the H & C and then on to the LSWR by using the connection north of Grove Road station. There was through booking from Richmond to the City. Thus the GWR reached Richmond, but only briefly, for the service was discontinued on 31 October of the same year. They had been standard gauge trains, because as already noted, broad gauge track was never laid beyond Hammersmith (it did get into south London, as far as Clapham Junction, but was never used there for regular services). From June to October, the LSWR diverted their trains over the new Chiswick curve to Hounslow, instead of Richmond; presumably the Great Western gave up due to lack of traffic.

But in early 1870s a new intruder appeared on the scene: the Metropolitan District Company, always colloquially called the 'District', in order not to confuse it with the Metropolitan Company. The District had pushed westwards from Earls Court and reached Hammersmith Broadway in 1874 (the first station was burnt down and was rebuilt in 1882).

The District were anxious to extend into the western and south-western suburbs, and therefore applied to Parliament for Powers to connect with the LSWR beyond Hammersmith Broadway and west of Grove Road station. The LSWR were against this, but they were even more opposed to the District's proposal to extend their line from Putney Bridge to Barnes, and thus get access to Richmond over the line from Waterloo. The LSWR were forced to accede to the granting of running

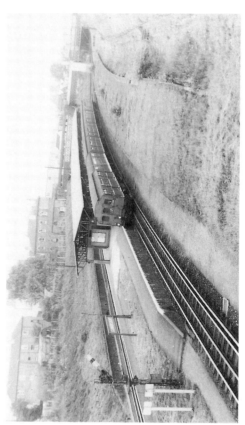

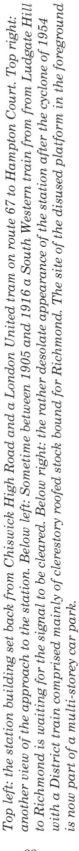

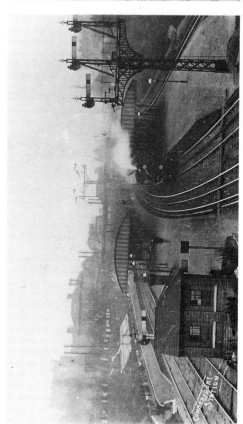

Top left: the station building set back from Chiswick High Road and a London United tram on route 67 to Hampton Court. Top right: another view of the approach to the station. Below left: Sometime between 1905 and 1916 a South Western train from from Ludgate Hill to Richmond is waiting for the signal to be cleared. Below right: the rather desolate appearance of the station after the cyclone of 1954 with a District train comprised mainly of clerestory roofed stock bound for Richmond. The site of the disused platform in the foreground is now part of a multi-storey car park.

powers from Hammersmith to Richmond, in return for which the District dropped the Putney Bridge-Barnes proposal; it was cheaper than bridging the Thames. Given that the Midland Railway financed the extension at Hammersmith, the District had come off well, and the LSWR had been out-manoeuvred. From this time their territorial position started to decline. The K & R, unlike the 1846 line from Clapham Junction to Richmond, had not been a success, and so giving the District running powers and collecting the revenue was one way of getting some return on their capital. The LSWR and the Midland were given running powers over the District line to Mansion House which was why the Midland built the extension, but for the LSWR this was a useless option, as it would not have been possible to fit in enough trains to earn any revenue. The Midland ran highly profitable coal trains to West Kensington and Kensington High Street depots.

The District's extension from Hammersmith was also in direct competition with the Metropolitan's services over the H & C from the City; the Met called it the "Hammersmith Aggression".

THE ARRIVAL OF THE DISTRICT

The District opened their Mansion House to Richmond service on 1 June 1877, and carried 54,000 passengers in the first month. This was a key event in Richmond's railway history and was welcomed by the travelling public of that time. The "Richmond and Twickenham Times" took the opportunity to review the town's railway services, and reported that there had "recently been a successful agitation for a more speedy and extensive service." [18] This presumably referred to improvements made by the LSWR in the mid seventies, and it was hoped no doubt that competition from the newcomer would encourage them to make more.

The LSWR had been notorious for bad timekeeping since its beginnings in the 1830s. An editorial in the Richmond and Twickenham Times had complained about the lateness of trains and suggested that a deputation of prominent citizens should be formed to present passengers' grievances to the LSWR. [19] A story is quoted about a porter, who when asked when an overdue train was likely to arrive, said:

> "That is very uncertain, she (the train) having only kept her time once during the last week, and that was a wonderful exception".
> This porter went on to say that in three years he hardly knew of a train that was not late! [20]

According to one writer, G.A. Sekon, the company had a good name for safety, and he said "it was this fact that largely developed the immense suburban residential traffic that really grew up on the railway. When taunted with the slowness of their trains, Mr Chaplin, the Chairman, invariably made the reply 'If we are slow, we are safe!' [21]

There had been published a report saying that a committee of season ticket holders, which was appointed at a meeting on 18 January 1877, had now met the General Manager of the LSWR, who had "introduced improvements" in the service. No details of these improvements are given in this article, though apparently the General Manager said that it was hoped that when the permanent way improvements between Clapham Junction and Waterloo are completed, services can be accelerated." [22]

A letter to the paper stated that District fares were on a similar level to the LSWR – but it was hoped that the District "can see their way to an early reduction". [23] The same correspondent said that there were 22 up and 23 down trains, taking 44 to 50 minutes for the journey to Mansion House. The annual season ticket was £17.10s (first class?), which was, apparently, £5 less than to Cannon Street on the LSWR. The carriages were described as "dingy", with no curtains because they had not previously been used on a "daylight" route.

In contrast to the LSWR route it was pointed out that the walk across Waterloo Bridge was now avoided, as was the need to change for Cannon Street at Waterloo. There had long been a feeling that Waterloo station was too far from the City, as previously noted. The article explained that passengers travelling by the District would be able to go "full dress" to the theatre, using such stations as Temple or Charing Cross (but starched white shirts might have suffered from smoke and smuts in the tunnels – the paper took this for granted). Looking to the future, the "Times" went on to say

Top: Richmond Bridge with a 4-VEP unit bound for Reading.

Centre: Kew with unusual elaborate gothic capitals and finials designed by W.R. Galbraith and opened in 1869.

Below: Kingston, similar in design to Richmond but disfigured by gas pipes.

that the new service would benefit Richmond "whose residential attractions are now brought within reach of thousands to whom they have not hitherto been readily available". [24]

The Metropolitan Company, rivals and competitors of the District, were not to be outdone by the District, and using their running powers over the K & R opened an hourly service from Aldgate to Richmond on 1 October 1877. Since Aldgate was further than Mansion House and the journey took longer, this service was probably not as well patronised as the District, but it lasted until 1906. It did mean, however, that a passenger at Richmond station had the choice of six routes to London:

Putney-Clapham Junction-Waterloo
Hammersmith-Kensington-Waterloo
Hammersmith-Kensington-Ludgate Hill
Hammersmith-Mansion House
Hammersmith-Paddington-Aldgate
Willesden Junction-Hampstead-Broad Street

By changing trains only once it would have been possible to get to London Bridge, Cannon Street, Fenchurch Street or Euston. No change of train was necessary for the other termini. This was the heyday of intensive steam suburban services; indeed, the Midland experimented with a Moorgate-St Pancras-Cricklewood-Richmond service in 1875-76. There were ten or eleven trains per day taking 50 minutes, with no second class accommodation, this company being the first to abolish it. The Midland also tried a St. Pancras-Cricklewood-Turnham Green-Earls Court service, but nobody wanted that either, and it was withdrawn by 1880. This enterprise and competition did stimulate the NLR into providing 3rd class carriages with sawdust on the floor and even produced some improvements in service from the LSWR. It will be remembered that the Midland ran coal trains from Cricklewood to Kensington; these were the only goods trains to use the K & R.

Relations between the LSWR and the District soon became strained. At this time it was LSWR practice for their platforms to be 1ft 9ins above rail level – lower than most companies, including the District. Their carriages were designed for platforms of 3ft 1ins. In September 1877 there was an accident at Gunnersbury, and as the Richmond and Twickenham Times pointed out, the carriages of the companies using the station (LSWR, District, and North London) all had running boards at different heights, the gap with the District coaches being the largest. The paper advocated replacement of the District rolling stock by carriages adapted for the K & R line, and standardisation amongst the three companies. [25] In April 1878 an elderly passenger was injured at Turnham Green whilst climbing into a District carriage. At the Board of Trade Inquiry the Railway Inspector recommended that the platforms were either raised, or the District carriages fitted with a footboard corresponding to the height of the platform. Probably little was done as the LSWR disclaimed any responsibility for the problem. On two days in March 1879 passengers were injured at Richmond whilst getting out of carriages; one of these accidents was fatal. Apparently, Richmond Vestry called for the raising of platforms, and minutes, albeit somewhat emotionally.:

"Any old woman at the Workhouse could have designed better and more convenient stations than those at Richmond. Even the old station . . . would anyone suppose that an engineer with any brains about him at all could have designed such a station?" [26]

Passengers were required to step down 2ft 6ins or even 2ft 10ins, and a case was reported of a lady being forced to sit on the carriage floor before lowering herself on to the platform. The Vestry referred the problem to the Board of Trade, who, not having received statutory notification of the accidents from the LSWR, summonsed the Company. After sending a deputation to the Board, charges were withdrawn on payment of costs. [27] What action either company took is not clear, and this may be an example of how railway companies sometimes evaded their social responsibilities, though from the evidence of later photographs, the LSWR standardised their platforms probably in 1878. British practice, as opposed to that in most other countries, was to have high platforms from the 1880s onwards, and these have remained to the present day.

On 1 July 1879 the District opened their Ealing service, the line from Turnham Green having been authorised two years bfore. The District were now the main users of the Hammersmith (Studland

Road junction) to Turnham Green section of the LSWR line. Their traffic increased more when the line from Acton Town to Hounslow opened in 1883 (this is now the Piccadilly line). In desperation the LSWR started a Gunnersbury-Brentford-Hounslow-Twickenham-Richmond-Gunnersbury service, but as nobody wanted it the service was withdrawn after a few months. The advantage that the District had, and about which the LSWR could do nothing, was that their line ran through the City and close to the West End, and so these services have not only survived, but continue to be important. Bradshaw in 1887 shows that there were 28 LSWR trains per day on the K & R, down and up, alternating between Waterloo and Ludgate Hill. The timetable allowed them 45 minutes to the former, and 65 minutes to the latter, but they probably took longer given the number of junctions they had to traverse, where they could have been delayed.

It is probable that the District services ran late, because of the congestion on the Circle Line, which was shared with the Metropolitan (from Cromwell Road junction to South Kensington, which is why there were four tracks). The circle had been completed in 1884, at vast expense, and after much quarrelling between the companies. The northern side and the City widened lines carried 900 trains a day, many of them goods. [28] As already noted, the Metropolitan had started a service from Moorgate St and Aldgate (to which the line had been extended in 1876), to Richmond, shortly after the District had started their service to Richmond. From May 1875 to February 1878, with the GWR, they had run a horse bus from Turnham Green to their Shepherd's Bush station on the H & C line. At this time the NLR ran an 'interval' service, for which they were renowned – a train every half hour from Broad Street to Richmond. As already suggested, Richmond station must have been busy from 1877 onwards, so much so that a further platform was added to the "new" station.

Trains of five companies could be seen there: LSWR, NLR, District, Metropolitan, GWR. The Midland put in a brief appearance. By today's standards these services were unattractive; slow, dirty, and uncomfortable on wooden seats in unsprung four wheel coaches, and also cold in winter. Also, railway travel was comparatively expensive in Victorian England. The Richmond and Twickenham Times had complained in 1873 that carriages for third class passengers could be described as 'cattle trucks', and said the railway should treat its best customers in a more reasonable way. [29] Between 1859 and 1873 the demand for third class travel had increased, and by 1878 provision was slightly better, for in December 1878 the paper exclaimed:-

> "Wonders will never cease. At last the South Western Railway have introduced something like a comfortable third class carriage on the Windsor line. At present, however, there are only a few of them, and their padded seats and backs are well sought after. Let me now express an earnest hope that the many cattle trucks which have so long served as 'thirds' on our local lines will quickly be driven to the breaking-up department, never again to be the cause of swearing and grumbling by discontented passengers, who very probably expect from the South Western as much comfort as they have ever been able to secure from other and more considerate companies – to wit the North London and the Midland." [30]

When considering these criticisms it is important to bear in mind that the services on offer were far better than anything that had gone before; the suburban steam trains may have averaged only 20mph, but that was three times faster than a horse-bus or a carrier's waggon. Richmond had more railway services than bigger towns elsewhere. Why was it so attractive to the railway companies? The answer may be that it had a proportionately large upper-middle, and middle class population, and what one writer called the "richer sort" of clerk [31] – the type of customers the railways wanted.

In 1873 "The Architect" opined that Richmond was now a middle-class suburb, and pointed out that whereas the upper classes and working classes do not move out to suburbs:-

> "The middle class we speak of, whose laudable ambition is to occupy, not lodgings furnished or unfurnished, but self-contained houses of their own, betake themselves to far-off spots like Richmond."

This periodical called them a "special middle class" of Londoners, whose incomes range from "three to five hundred a year." [32]

Added to this were the tourist attractions of the Park and the river, and so there was not only

Top: Hounslow loop train formed of a class 455 unit crossing Barnes Bridge. The first bridge was opened on 22 August 1849, designed and built by Joseph Locke and Thomas Brassey. The bridge was rebuilt in 1894/5 with new brick piers, wrought iron bowstring girders alongside the original, together with a pedestrian walkway. The LSWR ran trains on to the bridge using it as a grandstand to view boat races.

Left: The original entrance to Barnes Bridge station with the steps that now lead to the up platform and the footbridge across the river to the right.

Below: Barnes signalbox, opened in 1959, and the Loop line level crossing.

guaranteed business traffic during the working week, but leisure traffic at weekends and holidays. Richmond was the first town of consequence beyond the western edge of London, and was a logical terminus for suburban services. Another important factor was that the intervening districts of Chiswick, Acton, Barnes, Mortlake, as well as Twickenham, Strawberry Hill and Shepperton to the west, were filling up. They were the 'railway villages' described by James Thorn. [33] Indeed the whole of the west London area expanded residentially in the last quarter of the 19th century, as the railway companies had hoped: "brick terraces and pairs, semi-detached, so characteristic of the Victorian age". [34]

Symptomatic of this growth was the desire in 1873-6 for a station in the Ailsa Park area between Richmond railway bridge and Twickenham. In response to local pressure the LSWR agreed to build one – but only if the local community subscribed one third of the cost of £3000. The money was raised and St. Margarets station was opened in October 1876. It is close to Twickenham station, which explains the Company's reluctance. The Richmond and Twickenham Times complained about the state of Twickenham station, saying that no improvements had been made for the last 30 years (i.e. since it had opened), during which time "three branches" (Kingston, Shepperton, and Reading) had opened. The editorial stated that "Twickenhamites" should press for improvements, because "without exception the station is the most disreputable on this part of the South Western Railway".[35]

The population of Richmond had doubled between 1851 and 1881, from 9,255 to 19,068, as had the population of Mortlake, which had grown from 3,110 to 6,330. The population of Barnes had trebled from 1,879 to 5,999. Apart from any effects of the railway this factor must have also pushed up property prices, and the increase in population, in its turn, acted on the railway; because of housing expansion two new stations were opened on the Kensington and Richmond line. One was Shaftesbury Road, in 1873, but re-named Ravenscourt Park in 1888; the other was Shepherd's Bush, opened in 1874. This was to the south of the Green – there was already a Shepherd's Bush station to the west of the Green on the H & C line.

It is probable that the residential development here was stimulated by the railway. As Mr Jackson says:-

> "Although the housebuilding which had virtually shut in the line as far as Turnham Green by 1901 owed something to the horse tramways along the roads west of Shepherd's Bush and Hammersmith to Kew Bridge after 1882-3, it was primarily succoured by the increasing variety and intensity of the train services worked over the Kensington and Richmond (line)". [36]

Similarly, the opening of the District extensions to Ealing in 1879 and Putney Bridge a year later had seen a significant increase in house-building in those areas.

LSWR services were unchanged until 1906, when an additional Clapham Junction-Kensington-Richmond service, taking about 50 minutes, was provided. Also, from 1901 to 1909 a service from Clapham Junction to Twickenham, via Kensington, the Chiswick curve and Hounslow, was added. But as Mr Jackson says, the LSWR was now "very much the minor operator on its own line". [37] He also says that in the early 1900s there were 28 trains each way daily compared with 25 District, 17 Metropolitan/GWR, and 19 NLR.

On the line from Waterloo to Richmond via Putney, some services were improving: by 1904 timetables show 31 down steam trains on the Hounslow 'Loop' – but only the same number on the Kingston 'Roundabout' (which was not an improvement). At this time there were 22 down trains to Wimbledon via East Putney.

In 1885 the section of line from Putney to Barnes was quadrupled; to permit this the original Putney station was demolished, and alterations made at Barnes. Two years later the section from Clapham Junction to Putney was quadrupled; this section had taken longer as the viaduct over the Wandle and the cutting east of Putney had to be widened. The spur, with its flyover to East Putney was opened in 1889.

In the morning rush-hour trains were leaving Richmond for six destinations: Waterloo (two routes), Ludgate Hill, Broad Street, Aldgate, Whitechapel, and New Cross. The last named was an extension of the District sevice from Mansion House, via the East London line, and had started in

October 1884; Metropolitan trains from Hammersmith to New Cross had started at the same time. From 1902 to 1912 some of the West London extension services from Clapham Junction to Kensington were extended to Richmond and Kingston. An interesting aspect of the summer of 1907-8 was the LSWR service from Richmond to Ilfracombe, via Kensington and Clapham Junction. The idea of saving holidaymakers the necessity of travelling to Waterloo never caught on, and the service was abandoned after two seasons. There was also, from 1905 to 1908, a Midland Railway service from Bradford, Yorkshire, to Portsmouth via the NSWJR and Richmond.

Finally in this period, 1909, another development worth recording is that the NLR trains from Kew Bridge were diverted to Richmond, providing a half-hourly service. The NLR was now in decline, and was operated by the London and North Western (LNWR) from the same year, whose carriages were then seen in Richmond – the seventh company whose livery could be seen at that station. They must have been better than the 4-wheelers the NLR continued to use, within living memory, long after other companies had scrapped theirs.

In 1899 a cast-iron bridge at Norwood had collapsed. This threw doubt on the durability of cast-iron bridges, and as a result the LSWR decided to re-build, in wrought-iron, the river bridges at Barnes, Kingston and Richmond. The last was re-constructed in the years 1906-8, the LSWR Engineer being Alfred Szlumper of the LSWR, brother of Sir James Szlumper, also a railway engineer, and Mayor of Richmond in 1893, 1900 and 1904.

A WORD ABOUT STEAM ENGINES

"We may here mention as an interesting fact, that more than 300 trains leave Richmond on every weekday . . ." [38]

a) London and South Western

With the advent of the electric train and the end of the steam age at Richmond – earlier than in most places – something should be said at this point in the narrative about the steam locomotives that pulled trains in and out of Richmond. The first thing to be said is that they were small, diminutive, in fact. This can easily be seen from surviving photographs when the size of the locomotive is compared to the size of the human figure, i.e. its driver, or any other figures near it. They were "tank" engines, not express locomotives. Given that six different companies operated in and out of Richmond, there would, from the 1870s, have been a variety of locomotives around. No examples of these machines survived from the 1840s or 1850s, but an LSWR Beattie 'well' tank engine of the 1860s is to be found at the Buckinghamshire Railway Centre near Aylesbury. These locomotives worked suburban trains from Waterloo to Richmond, via Clapham Junction, and via Kensington, until the last decade of the Century. They were superseded by the bigger Adams 4-4-2 tank engines, because carriages were getting heavier as passenger accommodation improved (if only marginally). These machines were supplemented by Adams O2 class 0-4-4 tank engines, which were slightly smaller. Both classes survived until electrification; an example of the former is preserved in working order on the Bluebell Railway in Sussex, and there is an example of the latter working at the Isle of Wight Steam Railway. LSWR locomotives were painted light green.

b) North London

North London engines "while neat and symmetrical, were not beautiful but they were very efficient", [39] though some would argue that they were beautiful. Painted black they were also mainly 2-4-0 and 0-4-2s, and then later, 4-4-0 tank engines, built at the company's works at Bow. Although the company only owned 14 route miles of track, they worked over other companies' lines (e.g. the LSWR to Richmond) with intensive services, and so they maintained a prodigious stock of engines (24 in 1858, 66 in 1873, 104 in 1891, and 123 in 1908). William Adams was Chief Mechanical Engineer to the North London from 1854 to 1873, moving to the LSWR in 1878, where he worked until 1895. His influence on both companies was considerable, and the similarities between the two companies' locomotives can be seen. Adams' engines on both the LSWR and NLR had "open cabs, polished brass domes, copper-capped chimneys, and they were styled in a most ornate green livery". [40]

An interesting point is that the coal bunkers on NLR engines always remained inside the cab – even when the cabs became enclosed during the 1880s. The bunkers were of limited capacity and so may have been an incentive to economy on a line, which it has been said, put low consumption before punctuality: "The drivers made much use of falling gradients with steam shut off". [41]

In 1928, the last remaining 4-4-0 was earmarked for preservation, but the decision was reversed and it was broken up in 1932. However, one of the 0-6-0 tank engines designed by J.C. Park in 1879 for goods trains, has been preserved by the Bluebell Railway.

c) District and Metropolitan

The District locomotives were all of the same class. These were 4-4-0 tank engines built by Beyer Peacock and Company from 1871 to 1886. No cab was provided for the crew, though at some time towards the end of the century the weatherboard was bent back to give some protection from the elements. It has been said that the crews did not want covered cabs as they inhibited the dispersal of smoke in tunnels, but as the District expanded westwards and into the open air with its surface routes to Richmond and Ealing, some protection must have been needed. The photograph therefore probably dates from the turn of the century.

These machines were small even by the standards of the time weighing only 42 tons. The earlier ones had wrought iron boilers; later engines had steel boilers, with a higher working pressure. Steam exhaust was condensed by being passed into the cold water tanks (hence the term 'tank' engine) at the side of the boiler. Coke was used which reduced the output of smoke. The Company's stock of locomotives was 54; they were painted green, and were maintained and overhauled at the depot at Lillie Bridge, West Kensington.

Unsurprisingly, the Metropolitan also used the same class of locomotive, and as with the District this basic design was used until steam ended on the underground section forty years later. They were known as the A class, and B class – the latter having minor modifications. These locomotives also had no cab, only a weatherboard, though covered cabs were provide later. 148 of them were built between 1864-1885 for four different railways in London, the longest survivor lasting until 1948. On the Metropolitan these engines were painted olive green until 1885 when the Company's livery was changed to dark chocolate. The chimney tops were of burnished copper, and the steam domes had brass covers, but they were later painted over as they must have been difficult to keep clean. There were brass numerals at the front of the funnel. As with the District locomotives, large and prominent pipes carried cylinder exhaust to the top of the water tanks, in order to condense steam exhaust. The A class engines were given classical names:-

> No. 1 Jupiter
> 2 Mars
> 3 Juno
> 4 Mercury
> 5 Apollo
> 6 Medusa

and so on. It has, apparently, been suggested that the names bear a close resemblance to paintings in the Titian Gallery at Blenheim Palace, which were destroyed by fire in 1861: "It could well be that the publicity given to the loss of the paintings at the time suggested the names of these Greek gods and goddesses for the modern leviathans." [42] This explanation may be fanciful, for several railway companies, e.g. LSWR and GWR used classical names, especially in the 'heroic' or classic railway period 1830-1850. The A class locomotives supplied to the District and Metropolitan companies by Beyer-Peacock of Manchester, cost the former company £2280 each, whereas the latter company, for some reason, paid more – £2675 for each of the first thirty-three machines.

An example of a Metropolitan 'A' class engine survives in the London Transport Museum at Covent Garden.

Notes and References

1.   Building News, vol. 43, 1882, p.470.
2.   Williams, op.cit., vol. 1, p.176.
3.   Jackson, op.cit., p.74.

4. Williams, op.cit., vol.1, p.179.
5. For example: E. Course, London Railways, 1962, p.173.
6. H.P. White, London Railway History (vol.3 of Regional History of the Railways of Great Britain), 1971, p.130.
7. R.M. Robbins, Points and Signals, 1968, pp.228-9.
8. Hiscoke, op.cit., no.39, May 1866, p.198.
9. Jackson, op.cit., p.329.
10. West London Observer, 16 January 1869.
11. Jackson, op.cit., p.329.
12. B. Cherry and N. Pevsner, The Buildings of England, London 2: South, 1983, p.505.
13. J.C. Gillham, The Railways of Kew and Gunnersbury, Railway Magazine, August 1956, pp.503-4.
14. West London Observer, 16 January 1869.
15. E. Klapper, London's Lost Railways, 1976.
16. RH, 10 September 1938.
17. Jackson, op.cit., p.329.
18. RTT, 16 June 1877.
19. op.cit., 28 June 1877.
20. Ibid.
21. G.A. Sekon, London and South Western Railway, 1896, quoted by T. Sherwood in Wandsworth Historian, No. 42, September 1984.
22. RTT, 14 April 1877.
23. op.cit., 16 June 1877.
24. Ibid.
25. op.cit., 6 October 1877.
26. Quoted by Williams, op.cit., vol. 2, p.27.
27. Ibid.
28. J. Simmons, The Railway in England and Wales 1830-1914, 1978, p.123.
29. RTT, 7 June 1873.
30. op.cit., ? December.
31. W. Besant, London in the Nineteenth Century, 1909, p.29.
32. The Architect, vol.10, 1873, p.170.
33. See J. Thorne, Environs of London, 1876.
34. Simmons, op.cit., p.128.
35. RTT, 24 March 1877.
36. Jackson, op.cit., p.330.
37. Jackson, op.cit., p.332.
38. Simpson, op.cit., p.13.
39. R.M. Robbins, The North London Railway, 1983, p.22.
40. National Railway Musem, North London Railway – a pictorial record, 1979, p.xiv.
41. Ibid.
42. D. Edwards and R. Pigram, The Golden Years of the Metropolitan Railway, 1983, p.31.

Part IV
Electrification and the Twentieth Century System: 1905-1985

"The town is particularly fortunate in its railway service, the eight miles which divide it from the Metropolis being traversed by trains of no fewer than six Railway Companies. Waterloo can be reached in twenty minutes; and on Sundays omnibuses run to and from London. There is also a service of electric trams from Richmond Bridge to Hampton Court and Hammersmith; horse trams from Richmond to Kew, and an excellent service of omnibuses from Surbiton through Richmond to Ealing." [1]

By the early years of the Twentieth Century, most railway companies with suburban systems in London and the other major cities, were seriously worried about competition from electric trams. One of the first such services in London was opened by London United Tramways, in 1901, from Kew to Shepherd's Bush, parallel to the Kensington-Richmond line. This was followed by a Hammersmith-Hounslow service, which was later extended to Kingston. The LSWR loop line, on which the service was slow, infrequent, and therefore unpopular, lost traffic. London United also owned the horse tramway from Richmond to Kew, but for reasons which are not clear they abandoned this instead of electrifying it as planned.

The significance for Richmond of these developments was that the District responded to tram competition by electrification; it had an antediluvian stock of four-wheelers (the Metropolitan were using rigid eight wheelers) and was "suffering severely from hardened arteries". [2] However, the capital cost of electrification was high, and so far as the Kensington-Richmond line was concerned it was realised by both the District and the LSWR that segregation of District electric and LSWR steam services would be required to carry the intensive service that was planned. The section between Hammersmith and Turnham Green was now carrying 148 trains each way daily. Because of the cost quadrupling was postponed but electrification from Hammersmith to Richmond was completed by 1905. For the LSWR this was the only way the Kensington and Richmond line could survive (the District had electrified to Ealing, South Harrow, Wimbledon, and Hounslow, in the same year – a tremendous technical feat). The LSWR lines into Richmond were not electrified at this time, because competitive pressure on them was not so intense.

On 31 July 1905 the last steam train for Mansion House left Richmond; on the next day the electric service began – a significant development in the railway history of Richmond.

The four rail system for collection of current, with multiple units, was chosen. [3] The direct current four rail system was adopted by the District and Metropolitan companies following a Board of Trade inquiry and recommendation, because at first the companies had been unable to agree. The ouside rail is positive, the inside rail is negative or carries the return current. This system influenced the LSWR in their choice of a similar three rail system where one of the running rails is used as a negative. The rolling stock was of American design, owing much to American finance and technology, and based on the Brooklyn Elevated Railway. The carriages were open with rattan covered longitudinal seats, train sets consisting of seven cars, of which three were motors and four were trailers. The electrical equipment was supplied by the British Thomson-Houston Company, the cars being built by the British Electrical Engineering Company, and the Metropolitan Amalgamated Railway Carriage and Wagon Company. There was both first and third class accommodation, the opportunity being taken to dispense with second class but first class survived until the outbreak of the Second World War.

In 1920 all-steel carriages were introduced, which had neither the running-boards nor the clerestory-type roof of the earlier designs. Improved types were introduced in 1924, 1927 and 1931. The District replaced hand-operated doors by air operated doors in 1938. Designs were in advance of the other railway companies that still used wooden stock (and it is only within the last ten years that British Rail has introduced automatic sliding doors on trains to Richmond). Innovative facilities provided by the District, at Earls Court, included illuminated electrical indicators to let passengers know destinations of the next three trains.

There was an electric train every 15 minutes from Richmond, though by 1910 this seems to have been cut back to 30 minutes, possibly because of congestion on the K & R. Looking back in 1912, one of the local papers said:-

> "Richmond in fact owes a good deal of its increased prosperity in recent years to the efforts of the District Railway, which has brought it within easy reach of the greater part of London which lies north of the Thames". [4]

The LSWR steam service from Twickenham via Kensington to Waterloo and to Ludgate Hill had continued, though in 1908 the LSWR Chairman complained that 1½ million passengers had been lost to trams and buses in the previous six months. Continuing also were the ten Metropolitan steam and seven GWR steam services to Aldgate, also running at a substantial loss. The Hammersmith and City line was electrified in November 1906 and the last Metropolitan train left Richmond for Aldgate. The GWR stepped in to provide a steam rail motor (i.e. engine and carriage combined) from Ladbroke Grove to Richmond. This steam service was withdrawn at the end of 1910, finally ending the GWR association with Richmond.

Not unexpectedly, the Metropolitan then proposed an electric service of their own to Richmond; they were anxious to maintain their access to the town. Negotiations with the LSWR and District lasted until 1914, when the Metropolitan accepted arrangements with the District for through bookings to Richmond, via Hammersmith, receipts being guaranteed the Metropolitan. So finally ended that Company's association with the town after 30 years. As a result the connection between the H & C and the K & R was severed at the north end, in November 1914, and completely removed in 1916. It can be noted here that the H & C had been electrified, by the GWR, in 1906 (when the present Hammersmith station was built, as already noted, and the present carriage sheds constructed).

With the mixture of 400 steam and electric services daily crowding on to the Hammersmith-Turnham Green section of the K & R, the situation for the District became intolerable, as a contemporary depiction of these difficulties shows:

> "A [District] train coming from the City had its own troubles to overcome on its way to Ravenscourt Park, delays occurring from various causes in the tunnels. When it reached the London and South Western junction [Studland Road] it fell in with another train which had met with similar troubles on its way from Waterloo via the West London Railway and the Junctions. In consequence although in the timetables the trains did not clash, as a matter of fact they did, and the passengers were annoyed at the delay at that junction, where the [District] train had to start on a gradient of 1 in 50. The train had to wait its turn, and under the system of manual signalling about 5 minutes were wasted. When the train reached Turnham Green on its way to Ealing it was again unfortunate because it met a train on its way from Richmond, and before that train could be cleared further delay occurred. Another point to be borne in mind was that in booking the trains the South Western Railway Company always insisted, and rightly so, on clear booking both ways at the junction. Not only was the line to be clear in the direction in which the train was running, but it was also to be clear of the train coming up on the opposing line at the junction. Hence although theoretically a train was cleared every 4 minutes, in practice intervals had to be left, on account of trains which had nothing to do with District trains. In these

Above: London and South Western steam railmotor No. 3 leaving with a Twickenham to Gunnersbury service. The railmotors proved to be under-powered and were shortlived but the bodies were rebuilt as trailers for push and pull trains.

Below: An electric train comprised of two 3 car units arriving shortly after electrification, bound for Waterloo via Brentford.

H16 4-6-2 tank No. 30520. Similar to the G16 class, they were built for transfer freight trains from Feltham to Willesden, Brent and Nine Elms yards.

Adams' 0395 class was built between 1881 and 1886 and fifty were shipped to the Near East for war service in 1916-18. The last survivor was Feltham's No. 30567 (built in 1883 as No. 154) seen here on shed in 1955.

A mixed freight bound for Reading leaves Feltham marshalling yard behind N class 2-6-0 No. 31405 in 1962. No. D3495 is one of the diesel shunting locomotives that had superseded the G16 class by this time.

circumstances only about 10 trains per hour at the most could be run to the Ealing, Richmond, Hounslow and other lines, and as the traffic was expanding, the Traffic Department were at their wits' end to know what to do". [5]

The effect of electrification had been dramatic: in 1900 the District had been carrying 43.8 million passengers, the same as in 1886. By 1912 they were carrying upwards of 86 million". [6] By the early 1920s, they were again providing four trains an hour to Richmond, which was later increased to six.

The improvement in District services was also due to another factor however, the widening of the K & R. In 1910 they obtained a new agreement with the LSWR which provided for quadrupling of tracks between Studland Road junction, just west of Hammersmith, to just west of Turnham Green. Under this agreement the two tracks on the south side were to be for exclusive District use, together with the southern platforms at Turnham Green and Ravenscourt Park. Such details were agreed whereby the LSWR would control entrances and booking offices, but the two companies would employ their own station staff, including ticket collectors. Revenue from advertisements and automatic machines was divided up. But the main operational principle was that the District's electric passenger trains would be separated from the LSWR steam passenger trains.

The widening was carried out on the south side because land was cheaper, even though the configuration made for sharper curves. The work was carried out by the LSWR and took 15 months during which there was no interruption of traffic. The District lines from Hammersmith came in on the south side with no connection to the LSWR, so that Studland Road ceased to be a physical junction. Connection between the LSWR non-electrified and District electrified lines was west of Turnham Green, where a flyunder carried the up Richmond District line under the down Acton line, an arrangement which removed many of the previous delays. Here a new signal box was installed, one part of which operated the District's new Westinghouse high pressure electro-pneumatic system, [7] the other part of the signal box operating the LSWR Sykes manual "lock and block" system. The LSWR which had been technologically ahead in 1869, when the line opened, had now fallen behind.

Ravenscourt Park and Turnham Green were re-built with island platforms, and in 1912 the District opened a station for their own use on their leased tracks at Stamford Brook. The new tracks had come into use on 3 December 1911, and the result of the widening was that 610 trains per day could be accommodated, 278 of which were District, a 40% increase. Between 5.30pm and 6.30pm there were 26 trains in each direction. [8]

Faced with this competition, together with competition from electric trams and the new motor buses, the LSWR now began to cut back its steam services. The Richmond to Waterloo service was reduced to 13 trains a day, and the Ludgate Hill service to 10. From thereon the service declined remorselessly; there was one train daily from Clapham Junction to Richmond, and a limited service from Battersea (on the West London line) to Richmond. By 1912 the service to Waterloo (via Kensington) was cut back to Clapham Junction, and by 1914 there were only two trains daily between Richmond and Ludgate Hill; by 1915 only one. In this year the Richmond-Clapham Junction service was severely cut, and converted to push-pull operation with two coach sets. Then in June 1916 all LSWR services over the Kensington and Richmond line ceased; Shepherd's Bush station, Hammersmith Grove Road, and the northern platforms at Turnham Green and Ravenscourt Park were closed.

THE EFFECTS OF TUBE RAILWAYS

The Central London Railway had been absorbed by the Underground Group on 1 January 1913, and as already noted, abandoned its plans for extending into the Thames Valley. Authorisation to extend to Gunnersbury was granted in 1913 but was also allowed to lapse. Another attempt in the 1920s was a proposal to join the disused Kensington and Richmond about 300 yards west of Shepherd's Bush (LSWR). But the Great Northern, Piccadilly and Brompton (later known as the Piccadilly) got powers to use the LSWR tracks from Studland Road as far as Twickenham in 1913. This had the effect of keeping out the Metropolitan which had wanted to put on an electric service to Richmond.

Because the LSWR needed to widen their lines between Richmond and Twickenham to separate the electric trains, whether Central London or Piccadilly, they obtained powers, like the proposals above, on 15 August 1913, to provide four tracks and to reconstruct Richmond and Twickenham stations. As finally happened in 1954, the latter was to be re-sited to the east. Some land was acquired during 1914-1915, but nothing further was done, probably because of the war. In the 1920s the Underground Group lost interest in the Thames Valley, possibly because the LSWR electrified from 1916.

With the electrification of the North London, the bridge over the river at Strand on the Green had to be strengthened in 1922 to take the weight of their electric trains. To save manpower, LSWR and NLR staff had been combined at Richmond, Kew, Gunnersbury, and Kew Bridge, from mid 1918.

In 1925 the scheme to extend the Piccadilly westwards over the K & R was revived, using the LSWR disused tracks, the same Act giving the Piccadilly running powers to Richmond. Ownership of the K & R was now vested in the Southern Railway, as successor to the LSWR. Once all four tracks were electrified and under the control of the Undergound group, [9] the running arrangements were altered and the junction at Turnham Green re-arranged. Piccadilly trains started running on 4 July 1932 using the centre tracks to run non-stop to Acton Town (to where the quadrupling had been extended).

With the re-arangement of tracks at Studland Road, the junction with the LSWR could not now be restored without major engineering works. But instead of demolishing the old viaduct round to Grove Road, it was rebuilt to allow the new eastbound District track to pass under it at a long skew angle, thus preserving the road bed upon which a link to the H & C could have been laid. The viaduct was therefore restored. [10] In fact no tracks were ever laid on the altered bed, although it was kept clear, and repaired when a small bomb fell on it during the Second World War. But the lattice girder bridge and the station house were demolished in 1954, any idea of a connection between the District and Piccadilly and the H & C being abandoned. In 1937 a large block of flats had been built across the track bed on the east side of Shepherd's Bush Road. Some relics lingered on: today the western parapet of the bridge in Shepherd's Bush Road can be easily seen, and at Hammersmith the stump of the viaduct to the west of Grove Road, attractively covered in weeds and wild flowers, can be observed by the curious onlooker. Otherwise, the Kensington-Richmond line, as such, has passed into oblivion.

Amongst other changes, Gunnersbury station has declined in importance. With the closure of the Chiswick curve in 1932 it was reduced from four to two platforms. The refreshment room was closed, and the station was badly damaged by a small cyclone in 1954. In 1967 BR completed a new station with an 18 storey office block and the old LSWR station house was demolished. Only Kew Gardens survives as an example of a Victorian station on the K & R (though the street-level building at Turnham Green is original).

The K & R is of historical interest and significance far beyond its utility to its owners. It is a good example of how the Parliamentary process produced compromise between the competing interests, and regulated relations between them; in this case it helped produce the service the public needed – for a time. This did not always happen, and in the end the eastern section of the line succumbed to the greater flexibility of road transport. It succeeded in preventing the GWR from building their own line to Richmond, but the District prevailed eventually because they could carry traffic direct from the City and West End, a problem the LSWR never solved. Much of this traffic came from the West London area beyond Hammersmith, which grew after 1880. The electrification of the District exploited this, as we have seen, a lesson that was borne in on the NLR and the LSWR.

ELECTRIFICATION OF THE LSWR [11]

Meanwhile, dissatisfaction with the LSWR steam services in the Thames Valley had been building up. In 1911-12 the local councils of Weybridge, Sunbury, Hampton Wick, Twickenham, Molesey, and Teddington attempted to persuade the Central London Railway to enter the area and break the LSWR monopoly. As already noted, this company had had plans to run to Richmond via Gunnersbury, and they then applied to the LSWR for running powers over their metals to Shepperton. The LSWR retaliated by including Shepperton, Hampton Court, and the Hounslow loop in electrification plans which had been in gestation since the early 1900s. It then became apparent that the CLR's interest in the Thames Valley had merely been a tactical manoeuvre against the background of a merger with the Underground Group; once their terms had been agreed the local councils were dropped "like discarded toys". [12]

A deputation from these councils had visited the General Manager of the LSWR, who said he hoped a better service would be provided by electrification, and in late 1912 and early 1913 the company announced that the following routes would be converted, on which traffic worth £100,000 a year had been lost:-

> Waterloo-East Putney-Wimbledon
> Waterloo-Richmond-Kingston-Waterloo
> Shepperton (Thames Valley) line
> Hounslow loop

The third rail system with multiple units instead of locos was chosen which would allow interchange with the District, with whom there was expected to be connection and inter-running, for example from East Putney to Wimbledon. Despite the War, work went ahead, and electric services started on the Waterloo-East Putney-Wimbledon route on 25 October 1915; on 30 January 1916, the Kingston roundabout and the Shepperton line were converted and on 12 March the Hounslow loop was ready.

Various improvements to the infrastructure were made, for example, lighting on the stations from Richmond to Kingston was converted to electricity. A station at Barnes Bridge was provided (the bridge had been strengthened in 1894 into an iron cantilever, and the footpath added with new abutments). The station, with its elegant entrance blending with the terrace, was opened in 1916.

In order to economise on current, 'coasting' marks were provided at appropriate distances from stations, which showed the driver where to cut off power; these are white mounted diamond shaped plates, and some can still be seen. The actual stopping places at station platforms were indicated by blue enamelled metal plates with white figures 3 and 6. Stations were given glass nameboards, on which the name was shown in white block letters on a blue panel with a white margin; these were lit from above at night.

As an economy new rolling stock was not constructed; instead steam stock was converted, at Eastleigh works. Three-coach units were used, the centre coach being a trailer with no motors (after 1920 two trailers were inserted between the two units to give eight car trains in peak hours). An innovation for the LSWR was the abolition of second class, and only a quarter of the seats were first class, which had dark blue cloth, with side and three intermediate arm-rests. In some units the first class accommodation was arranged as a saloon (having been converted from three second class compartments). The thirds were in red and black, and all compartments had two lights with opal glass bowls. The outsides of the coaches were painted dark green, lined in black and yellow. Destination discs were no longer used – as they had been on the front of steam engines – and instead a stencil plate with a letter route headcode was mounted in front of an opal glass panel, which was illuminated at night. The headcodes were:

> V Waterloo-Kingston-Richmond-Waterloo
> S Waterloo-Kingston-Shepperton
> S̲ Waterloo-Richmond-Shepperton
> V̄ Waterloo-Richmond-Kingston-Waterloo
> O Waterloo-Richmond-Hounslow-Brentford-Waterloo
> O Waterloo-Brentford-Hounslow-Richmond-Waterloo

Trains ran on a fixed interval basis, so that Richmond had six trains an hour to Waterloo, and six from Waterloo, four of which were via the Kingston 'roundabout', and two via the Hounslow 'loop'. There was a dramatic reduction in travel times – on average about one-third. For example, Teddington-Richmond-Waterloo had taken from 40 to 49 minutes, and now only took 32 minutes. Equally dramatic was the increase in traffic, which from 1913 to 1920 more than doubled, from 25 million passengers a year, to 52.6 million (but lower than the District's total of 86 million).

A FURTHER WORD ABOUT CARRIAGES

"No Feet Warmers will be supplied to Passengers in Trains which travel a distance less than 30 miles". [13]

Mention has already been made from time to time about carriages, but it is worth saying more because this is the item of equipment on a railway with which the passenger gets most closely acquainted, and together with time-keeping on which an opinion of the railway is generally based. But it is a neglected aspect of railway operations, on which the literature is sparse.

Suburban working called for the maximum number of passengers being put in to the largest number of carriages which would fit platforms, with minimum provision for luggage. In the last quarter of the 19th Century the number of carriages was maximised by close-coupling, and short buffers to save space. So carriages were kept in sets, generally of four-wheel vehicles, and the sets varied from four to fifteen vehicles. Early sets had a high proportion of firsts and seconds because many potential third class passengers were being carried in workmen's trains (or not at all). Unfortunately little evidence remains to tell us what type of train was used on suburban workings before block sets appeared in the 1870s. After the 1870s the proportion of thirds rose to three quarters of available seats, second class was abolished, and the LSWR, for example, progressed from four to six-wheeled stock.

a) London and South Western

From a Board of Trade Report [14] on an accident outside Waterloo on 10 December 1890, in thick fog, when a light engine struck the 6.25pm to Kingston, we get some idea of the composition of what may have been a typical suburban train at this time: according to the Report the Kingston train consisted of:-

> brake van with third class compartments
> third class carriage
> second class carriage
> first class carriages (two)
> brake vans with third class compartments (two)
> composite with compartments of different classes
> first class carriages (two)
> second class carriage
> third class carriages (two)
> brake van with third class compartments

This train was of fourteen vehicles in all, probably six-wheelers, and all fitted with automatic vacuum brake. From 1903, longer, bogie coaches began to appear on LSWR suburban services, but in the years prior to electrification the Company invested little in steam suburban stock. Despite the improvements of the late 1870s, 'demoted' main line coaches from the mid-Century had been used. Public pressure to improve second and third class accommodation had always been resisted with the argument that this would encourage passengers to forsake first class.

Oil pots in the roofs were the normal form of lighting until the 1880s when gas was introduced; keeping the pots refilled and the wicks trimmed in the long winter evenings and mornings must have been hard work. Coaches were painted in a singular livery: "the effect was of smoked salmon pink above the waistrail, and dark brown below, though the salmon colour was an illusion produced by buff paint and red lining.". [15]

b) North London Railway

Once again, not a lot is known about the rolling stock, though it lasted into living memory. The Company always used high roof four-wheelers until the end of its existence, and this included new stock constructed for the Richmond service in 1910. Trains were made up in close-coupled sets of eight, nine, ten, and twelve carriages. It seems likely that third class accommodation was not introduced on the Richmond service until 1878, and then, as with other companies, the floors of the compartments were covered in sawdust.

The NLR was the first line to use coal gas lighting in its carriages, from 1862, the gas being stored in large flexible containers in the guard's and luggage vans, in which passengers were not permitted to travel. Subsequently steel gas cylinders were fitted to the underframe of the carriages. The containers were replenished by flexible connections when the trains were standing in Broad Street.

The NLR was also the first company to introduce continuous brakes, i.e. a brake on every wheel of the train, in 1855. Various types of brake systems were tried, and the spirit of experimentation is caught by Michael Robbins:-

> ". . . it was not until after trying Miles' steam, Jackson's hydraulic, Clark's connected, Chambers' connected, Keys' connected, Chaplin's electric, and Clark's chain brakes, that in 1873 the Clark and Webb chain brake was adopted." [16]

This was displaced, however, by order of the Board of Trade in 1891, by the automatic vacuum.

The Company's livery was varnished teak; the brake vans had red ends. As trains were made up in sets, the first, second and third class compartments always stopped opposite the relevant signs for them at North London stations. Because of the density of their traffic the NLR tickets were printed with large black numbers for ease of station identification; those issued at Broad Street were numbered 1, Richmond's were 29. The Company installed the first automatic ticket machine at Broad Street in 1894.

With electrification in 1916, new and modern three-car units were introduced, using the direct current fourth rail system, which allowed through running to Richmond over the LSWR from Gunnersbury. The motor units were built by the Metropolitan Carriage, Wagon and Finance Company between 1914 and 1923. Electrical equipment was supplied by the Oerlikon Company, and the sets were known as 'Oerlikon stock', or just 'Oerlikons'. Loading was slow as they only had doors at the end of each carriage but they were represented as a great improvement on the old steam stock. They lasted until 1957-60, when they were replaced by three-car units built at Eastleigh.

c) District

Up to electrification in 1905, all coaches were four-wheelers. First class coaches had four compartments seating five a side, and second and third class had five compartments also seating five a side. The first class seats were upholstered; third class had only a strip of carpet on the seat and the back. Trains generally consisted of nine coaches; two firsts, three seconds, four thirds. Lighting was by coal gas carried in bags on the roofs, which was fed from mains at Mansion House and High Street, Kensington. In 1878 compressed oil gas was substituted – ahead of the LSWR who were still using rape oil in pots. The livery was varnished wood. The rolling-stock introduced from 1905 has already been described.

d) Metropolitan

This company regarded itself as superior to the District, used eight-wheel carriages in the 19th Century, and these could be seen at Richmond from October 1877 onwards. A photograph of them at Hammersmith in the 1880s is in existence. They were large and roomy "so that it was possible for a six-footer in a top hat to stand up in the centre of a compartment without embarrassment". [17] These carriages were of varnished teak, but painted white above the waist rail, which must have been difficult to keep clean. The first class had four side seats in well padded blue cloth, with carpeting on the floor. The second class had a strip of American cloth on the seats, and third class had bare varnished planks. Lighting was by coal gas carried in rubber bags in wooden boxes on the roof. A final point – inside door handles were fitted in the 1880s – after the District had adopted them.

DEVELOPMENTS IN THE INTER-WAR YEARS

In 1923 the LSWR and the Brighton and Chatham companies were amalgamated into the Southern Railway Company (SR), which vigorously pursued the policy of electrification, firstly in the suburban area, and then into the Home Counties. Electrification to Windsor was introduced from 6 July 1930, and such was the intensity of the service that seventeen trains in total were leaving Waterloo between 5pm and 6pm calling at Richmond. On the same date North Sheen and Whitton stations were opened, the former with a concrete 'island' platform, of a design and style used all over the Southern Electric system (as it was called) in its modernisation schemes.

On weekdays a service of trains from Waterloo to Windsor was provided every half-hour, which were fast to Richmond, taking 14 minutes, then stopping at all stations to Windsor, with an overall journey time of 46 minutes. In peak hours there was a train every 20 minutes, two of which were fast to Richmond, while the third ran via the loop, but not stopping until Feltham. The purpose of this must have been to ease congestion on the Richmond line. On Sundays there was a half-hourly service, with a stop at Clapham Junction. In 1933, the District Railway, together with the Underground Group, the Metropolitan, and the tube railways were absorbed into the London Passenger Transport Board.

As part of the Southern Electric modernisation programme a start was made at long last on rebuilding Richmond station in November 1935; the hitherto separate 'old' and 'new' stations were integrated as one, the ex-LSWR station being re-sited to the east of Kew Road, with 600 foot platforms. Cherry and Pevsner describe the station building, as always, succinctly:

"Portland stone, with some Scandinavian features. Lofty booking hall" [18]

Professor Simmons had described this and other stations on the Southern Electric system as "monuments of the early Jazz Age . . . they were cleaner, and easier to keep clean, than their predecessors". [19] Architecturally he feels there is little to praise them for, but the Builder disagreed, saying that both Surbiton and Richmond stations:

". . . show how admirably the Southern Railway have applied modern design and construction to their proper ends. They are to be congratulated on the results. All unnecessary fussy details, often so prominent in the past have been eliminated, reliance being placed on good lines and general good proportions." [12]

The main contractors were F.G. Minter of Putney.

Almost exactly 91 years after the first train had arrived in Richmond, the new booking hall was opened on 1 August 1937. The following day was a Bank Holiday. A local paper reported:

"Richmond station dealt with a record number of people – so far as an August Bank Holiday is concerned – on Monday, when no fewer than 80,000 tickets were collected. The visitors started to arrive before nine a.m. and many alighted from trains as late as five p.m. Between those hours 204 trains, at the rate of 38 an hour, set down passengers. At a conservative estimate, the number of people who came to Richmond by train from Friday evening last week to Monday evening was 150,000. Sunday saw an influx of 40,000". [21]

At St. Margarets, the signal box had been opened in 1882, and closed on 10 November 1974. In recent times Richmond bridge has undergone major repairs requiring single line working: the up line was used from 6 November 1983 to 25 February 1984. The down line was used to 13 May 1984 when normal working was resumed.

Electrified services began to Reading on 1 January 1939, with a train every 20 minutes in peak hours, and 30 minutes otherwise; there were now two outer suburban services, one to Staines which then split into a Windsor portion, and a Weybridge portion. The other service was to Ascot which then split into a Reading portion and an Aldershot/Guildford portion. Thirty six electric trains from Waterloo to Reading replaced twenty steam trains; the average travelling time was reduced by 11 minutes, but with more stops. By July 1939, twenty one trains were leaving Waterloo between 5pm and 6pm for the Richmond line; there were thirteen per hour outside peak times.

SOME POST-WAR EVENTS

There was a serious accident at Barnes on 2 December 1955. A goods train from Battersea Yard to Brent, which had been held at signals on the down local line, was re-starting when the 11.12pm Waterloo-Windsor train ran into the back of it, travelling at about 35mph. The two leading coaches of this train, the brake van and two wagons of the goods train were derailed; fire broke out consuming the first passenger coach and three wagons. Thirteen people were killed, including the driver of the electric train and the guard of the goods. Thirty-nine passengers and two policemen, assisting in rescue work, were injured.

In his Report, the Inspecting Officer of Railways blamed the signalmen at Point Pleasant junction (between Wandsworth and Putney), and the signalman at Barnes Junction box, for allowing the electric train to reach Barnes. They were also blamed for not switching off the current sooner, the fire having been caused by electric arcing. It was recommended that the colour-light signalling scheme for this section of line should be revived; this was brought into use on 22 February 1959. The signal box at Putney was closed, and three cabins at Barnes were replaced by the present panel box at Barnes junction but boxes at level crossings were retained to operate them. Barnes Coal yard lasted until 23 March 1969.

In 1939 work started on replacing Twickenham station and providing colour light signalling it was soon stopped by the Second World War. The new station, on a new location east of London Road, was not completed until 28 March 1954; five platforms were provided (two primarily for handling the rugby traffic which still brings vast crowds to important matches) instead of the previous three. Colour light signalling had to wait for the commissioning of the Feltham signal box, which now controls the Richmond and Loop lines from Barnes westwards to Wokingham, on 10 November 1974.

At Feltham the marshalling yard closed on 2 March 1969 and the locomotive depot which, it will be remembered, had taken over from Strawberry Hill, closed on 1 August 1970.

Richmond old goods depot had been taken out of use in November 1936, being replaced by the yard on the 'up', or north, side, but this was closed in September 1968. At the same time the siding to the Borough Council depot was closed. The gas works siding was closed in 1970, and in December 1972 the junction linking the North London lines to the Southern was taken out of use. Then in November 1974, Richmond signal box, opened in January 1940 and an excellent example of Southern restrained art deco or 'Odeon' architecture, was closed for the ex-LSWR lines, and controlled the ex-NLR lines only. All remaining sidings were removed from 24 February 1980. There is still a trailing connection between the ex-LSWR up line from platform 2, to platform 3, used by North London Line trains.

The level crossing gates at North Sheen were replaced by automatic lifting barriers on 11 November 1973; [22] at Barnes the gates on the Richmond line were replaced by barriers on 28 March 1976. On the loop line they were replaced on the 16 April of that year. The gates at Mortlake were replaced by a two barrier arrangement on 2 June 1974, but this was changed to four barriers on 5 October 1980. At White Hart Lane the gates were replaced and the signal box closed on 19 December 1976. From that date all these level crossings have been monitored by closed circuit television at Barnes signal box. What would the writer to The Times of 29 June 1846 have said about that?

THE HOUNSLOW 'LOOP' TODAY

When opened in 1849 this line followed a coaching route, and which was itself later supplanted by another form of road transport – the electric tram. But the western part of it was useful for goods coming off the NSWJR and going to Feltham yard. It is surprising how much of the original infrastructure survives. Chiswick (Grove Road) still has the original station house on the east side. Although there is now no sign of Chiswick east curve (up to Gunnersbury) which was removed in 1932, and on the site of which flats have been built, the track and platforms are still 'in situ' on the 1862 Kew curve at Kew Bridge station.

The NSWJR has survived still being used for north-south freight services though of less importance since the 1960s, when Feltham yard was closed. Now it comes into the loop with one track. There were wooden platforms at Isleworth until recently, and the station buildings, in Mr Jackson's words "gabled and barge-boarded, survive almost unaltered together with some of the Victorian villas that followed them". Before the villas, Isleworth had been an area of market gardens renowned for its raspberries and strawberries.

At Brentford the small goods shed still stands, and the embankment of the GWR branch line to Brentford Dock can still be seen. The coal yard sidings at Hounslow, originally a market town, have been removed and replaced by new housing, but the original superb LSWR station house and platform canopy with wooden columns survive, an excellent example of an early LSWR country station. Indeed, the old Richmond station may have looked like this. Even in the late 1980s, long after electrification and with frequent services, the loop still slumbers on, with a faintly rural charm; a goldmine for the railway archaeologist.

It is generally agreed that the 1960s were a revolutionary period in railway history – the transformation from the Victorian steam locomotive railway to the modern railway. Richmond railways, already electrified, were still affected by this change; in this decade goods and freight services virtually disappeared. The steam locomotive, of course, completely disappeared. On the ex-LSWR lines passenger services – especially for 'commuters' – were maintained, with Southern Region attempting to provide a railway service compatible with modern needs. Major timetable revisions were made in 1958 and 1967, and a new facility for passengers, a Travel Centre, was opened at Richmond Station in 1985 (but closed in 1990).

All post-war events, however, were overshadowed by the Beeching onslaught in 1963 on the old North London line – or Broad Street line as everyone called it – which had served Richmond since 1858. The spirited and energetic defence of this line which followed, and lasted well into the next decade, forms the concluding section of this essay.

Notes and References

1.   Where to Live Round London – Southern Side, 1907, p.138.
2.   White, op.cit., p.92.
3.   Information in the next two paragraphs is from C.E. Lee, The Metropolitan District Railway, undated, pp.36-7.
4   Richmond and Twickenham Times, 19 October 1912.
5.   Paper given by E.A. Ogilvie: The London and South Western and Metropolitan District Railways widening between Acton Lane and Galena Road; reply of W.E. Blake, proceedings of Institution of Civil Engineers, vol.192 (1913), p.157.
6.   Ogilvie, op.cit., p.164.
7.   Ogilvie, op.cit., Reply of Blake, p.157 who also suggested that had the automatic signalling been installed first, it might have made the widening unnecessary.
8.   Ogilvie, op.cit., p.157.
9.   Consisting of the District, London Electric (Piccadilly), Central London, and City and South London (now the Northern line).
10. J.C. Gillham, The Railways of Kew and Gunnersbury, Railway Magazine, September 1956, p.622.
11. For a full and detailed narrative of the electrification of the LSWR see G.T. Moody, Southern Electric, 1909-1979, 3rd edn., 1979, on some of which my account is based.
12. Jackson, op.cit., p.69.
13. Timetables of the London and South Western Railway and Steam Packets, November 1859.
14. South Western Circular, vol. 7, no.1, January 1986, pp.11 and 15 (Journal of the London and South Western Society).
15. C. Heap and J. van Riemsdijk, The Pre-Grouping Railways, part two, 1980, p.8.
16. R.M. Robbins, The North London Railway, 1983, p.24.
17. Jackson, op.cit., p.36.
18. Pevsner, op.cit., p.521.
19. J. Simmons, The Railways of Britain, edn. 1968, p.105.
20. The Builder, 25 March 1938, p.594.
21. RH 7 August 1937.
22. Much of the information in this section is obtained from G.A. Pryer, Track Layout Diagrams of the Southern Railway, Section 8, Windsor Lines, 1984, p.16.

RICHMOND TODAY

Top: The New station has changed little when compared with the photographs on pages 8 and 9. There are two North London trains formed of class 313 units and a District train of D78 stock.

Left: The entrance of the Southern Railway's booking hall, completed in 1937.

Below: The Windsor line platforms that replaced the Old Station in 1937.

The 1954 built station at Twickenham in 1985 before its recent refurbishment.

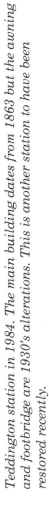

Teddington station in 1984. The main building dates from 1863 but the awning and footbridge are 1930's alterations. This is another station to have been restored recently.

Street level entrances: St. Margarets in 1991.

Part V
The North London Line

"May God save the Old North London" (Sir John Betjeman)

Little has been said in previous chapters on developments on the North London Railway because it is more convenient to treat it separately. it will be remembered that services from Fenchurch Street to Kew Bridge started on 1 August 1853; from May 1858 these were extended to Richmond and Twickenham, trains undergoing the time-consuming and cumbersome operation of reversing at Kew and Barnes, until the new curves were opened in February 1862. In July of the following year trains ran on to Kingston.

Because of congestion between Camden and Willesden on the LNWR main lines, a new line, called the Hampstead Junction Railway (the present line running through Gospel Oak and Hampstead Heath) opened in January 1860, along which Richmond trains were routed (and have been ever since). This line crossed over the LNWR main line on a bridge, on which six years later Willesden Junction High Level station was opened. For the first few years the service seems to have consisted of four trains per day in each direction, but after 1858 this was probably increased; possibly some trains terminated at Kew Bridge. The extension from Dalston to Broad Street built at a cost of £1.2 million was opened by the Lord Mayor and Sheriffs of the City on 31 October 1865. The station, on the edge of the City, and the extension were known thereafter as the "happy afterthought" – based, allegedly, on a comment by one of the North London directors, probably because the new line doubled their traffic: in 1866 the Company carried 14 million passengers; by 1880 this had risen to 32.7 million.

At the other end of the route, the LSWR's line from Acton Junction to Gunnersbury opened on 1 January 1869, as already mentioned, giving the North London a direct route to Richmond. At the same time services from Fenchurch Street to Richmond were discontinued, and the service through to Kingston was cut back to Richmond. From the opening of Broad Street station a fifteen minute interval service was inaugurated by the North London, a regularity on which they were always to pride themselves (as they did on the standardised order of carriages on the trains) which left Broad Street as follows:

> 10 minutes past the hour to Kensington, via the West London line
> 25 minutes past the hour to Kew Bridge
> 40 minutes past the hour to Kensington
> 55 minutes past the hour to Richmond

Therefore, whilst there was a generous "middle circle" service to Kensington (which was then on the western edge of London) operated by the LNWR, there was now only an hourly service to Richmond. This lasted down to 1909, when Kensington and Kew trains were diverted to Richmond, in the hope of recapturing lost traffic; a "shuttle" service took what passengers there were from Acton to Kew Bridge.

Around 1862 interchange tickets between the LSWR and North London had been available, but some time later this facility was withdrawn. The North London had always been slow to introduce third class compartments, but the short-lived Midland service from St Pancras to Richmond in 1875 had provided third class travel, which encouraged the North London to offer this facility. The only other improvement on the North London was the quadrupling of the line between Camden Road and Dalston in 1871. Probably this reduced delays rather than eliminated them.

In a sense the success of the North London was its downfall; the Company became complacent and ossified and unable to make progressive change. It will be recalled that the District and the Metropolitan electrified in 1905; the North London considered electrification in 1904, and again in 1908, but could not take the plunge until 1911, when work was started. Even then delays due to the First World War prevented electric services from starting until 1 October 1916, in the middle of the War. The electrification was carried out by the LNWR as part of their suburban programme, which included fourth rail electrification from Euston to Watford. This still exists, running parallel to the overhead electrification of the 1960s. The journey time from Broad Street to Richmond was cut by 12 minutes, to 44 minutes, not far short of the service that existed when Broad Street closed in 1986. The new rolling stock used has already been described.

Between the Wars services were gradually improved, but with the outbreak of hostilities again in 1939, some reductions were made. At one period of the War passenger services were withdrawn to allow greater utilisation for goods trains to and from the Docks, the service to Kew Bridge ceased for ever on 12 September 1940. After 1945, the pre-war service was restored, with minor changes, and this lasted until 1962. But during the 1950s traffic declined further; this was attributed to the 1952 fare increases, which were based on distance rather than competitive routes. The decline was also due to increasing car ownership, noticeable particularly at weekends. Staff reductions were made during this period, but on the other hand some of the stations were renovated.

Rumours of closure, although denied by British Railways, circulated in the summer of 1962; in September of that year the frequency of trains was reduced from four to three per hour, and all services after 9pm were withdrawn. The bombshell came with the publication of the Beeching Report in March 1963 which recommended withdrawal of the Broad Street-Richmond service.

After 100 years, what had brought the last surviving service of the North London to such a plight? As already suggested, decline had started as long ago as the end of the Nineteenth Century. From 1896 when the North London carried 46.3 million passengers, decline had been relentless; by 1910 passengers carried had dropped to 30 million, and by 1920 12 million (in 1987 it was 12 million). The inescapable fact was that the North London tank engines, with their rakes of four-wheel gas-lit wooden carriages, charming though they looked, could not compete with electric suburban trains, which were cheaper, nor with electric tubes, which were faster. Most telling of all, they could not compete with electric trams, which were more convenient.

From 1900 onwards developing electrified services have diverted radial traffic away from the North London:

> Northern line from Hampstead
> Bakerloo line – now Jubilee – from West Hampstead
> Piccadilly line from Acton and from Caledonian Road
> Victoria line from Highbury
> BR Great Northern electrics from Highbury
> BR Midland electrics from West Hampstead

As explained, the North London had hesitated too long over electrification; they should have electrified at the same time as the District and the Metropolitan, in 1905 and certainly no later than the LBSCR with their South London route in 1909. When it did come, electrification produced more traffic, but the North London never recovered the glory of its golden years of 1865-1895. Then it had been a pioneer orbital service, linking east, north, and west London i.e. much of London north of the river.

All along the North London route – at Richmond, Willesden, Hampstead, Hackney and elsewhere, a spirited and effective campaign of protest at the proposed closure was organised. After protracted parliamentary argument on 21st June 1965 it was announced by L.M. Region of B.R. that passenger services to Richmond would continue. However, in the light of further BR pruning in the 1970s it was necessary to resuscitate the campaign. By 1985 the future of the service seemed more secure with the electrification of the route from Dalston to North Woolwich, and the diversion of trains away from Broad Street to the latter station – forming the North London Link service.

When the handsome Oerlikon stock which had served the line for so long at last became life-expired it was replaced in 1957 by the 501 class emus which were little-loved – perhaps the three protective bars fitted to each droplight of the 501s produced a feeling of imprisonment which was not relieved by the then deplorable condition of the stations on the route. In 1985 the 501s gave way in their turn to SR Bulleid-style EPB units. By Spring 1990 altogether more enticing class 313 three car units superseded the EPBs.

Sadly, Broad Street station was demolished by property developers in 1986, its former greatness completely forgotten. For the sake of nostalgia it is worth recalling that the North Woolwich line is older than the North London. It opened in 1847, a year after the Richmond Railway, and the Italianate terminus has been turned into a charming museum of the Great Eastern Railway, one of the five different railway companies which have used the line over the past 143 years.

It seems that continued vigilance may be required by those who 'love the old North London! On the last day of 1991 the London "Times" had a prominent article 'To Brussels via Kew' – 'hopes for the often-threatened but indispensable North London line! Cynics may feel that this glance at the future appears somewhat optimistic since for the Winter of 91/2 BR has for the first time in years suspended Sunday services for several months. Observers have found it difficult to find the engineering work in progress which was the reason advanced for the closure.

Conclusion

This survey is not complete. There are many gaps in the story, and aspects where more research is needed. For example, it would be interesting to know who, apart from the LSWR, put up the capital for the Richmond Railway Company, in 1844-5. Also there is little here, as in most railway histories, about goods and freight services – a much neglected topic. Although heavy bulk materials could be brought to Richmond on the river, other merchandise must have come by railway, to be carted from the station by horse-drawn waggon and van.

It is important to challenge the assumptions which become part of the wisdom of railway historians; for example, it is generally assumed that the GWR discontinued their service to Richmond in 1870, after only four months, through lack of support. But until we actually know this can only be a hypothesis, which would be well worth testing by further research, because there may have been more interesting reasons. It may be that there were operational problems, particularly at Bishops Road (Paddington); it may be also that the strained relations between the GWR and the Metropolitan companies prevented the service from running on to the City – where it might have been better supported.

Local research is needed on the problem of the relationship between railways and suburban growth. This is especially so for Teddington and Strawberry Hill, where it is assumed that the railway created housing development, whereas only the ability and willingness of proprietors to sell land permitted this.

Richmond still has an excellent railway service, and to complete the story to date it is worth recording, that in the winter of 1991-92, there are seven trains an hour "up" from Richmond to Waterloo, and vice-versa. Of the "down" trains, two are for Reading, two for Windsor, two for Staines, two for Kingston and one for Guildford. The fastest Waterloo-Richmond timing is 15 minutes. Trains for Shepperton continue to be routed via Kingston at the rate of two per hour, taking 44 minutes from Waterloo; in the peak hours an additional service runs via Richmond. The Kingston 'roundabout' service which had long been discontinued outside peak hours was revived in the Summer of 1991 thanks to a subsidy by Kingston Council, worried at the town's decline. On the 'loop' weekday services have been re-organised, and there is a new off-peak service of two trains per hour to Hounslow, one train per hour of which runs on to Chertsey and Woking. At peak times there are two trains per hour, which from Hounslow return to Waterloo via Twickenham and Richmond. This means that Richmond has ten trains per hour at peak times.

District line trains leave Richmond every 7 minutes at peak times, and every 12 minutes off-peak, taking 38 minutes to reach Mansion House, their original 19th century destinations en-route to Barking or Upminster. North London Line trains leave every 20 minutes and reach North Woolwich in 65 minutes.

All these timings are vastly superior to those of the 1860s: one wonders what Hiscoke and Sons would have had to say about them in their Richmond Notes.

Appendix A

List of members of the Provisional Committee in the Prospectus of the Richmond and West End Junction Railway:

Sir George Larpent, Bart	Roehampton	W. Bland	Chislehurst
Hon. C.P. Williers, MP	Richmond	James Smith	Richmond
Will. Sargent	Putney Heath	Thomas Long	Richmond
Will. Price	Richmond	James Davy	Richmond
Richard Norman	New Broad Street	Will. Hawes	Lambeth
Henry Cornfoot	Richmond	Henry Weston	Borough Bank
John Brown	Portman Square	Henry Lewis Smale	Doctor's Commons
Stephen Phillips	New Broad Street	Martin Stutely	Regent's Park
John Dawson Lowden	Fleet Street	G.S. Kempson	Mortlake
Joseph Ellis	Richmond	Edward Scard	Kew
T.B. Simpson	Brixton	W. Cory	Battersea
Edward Collins	Richmond	Robt. Smith	Richmond
G. Vaughan	Regent's Park	W. Fletchney Black	Wilton Place

Other officials listed are:

Trustees:
Sir Thomas N. Reeve   Richmond
Benjamin Cohen   Richmond
Engineer:
George Parker Bidder
Solicitors:
Messrs Roy, Blunt & Co.   Lothbury
William Chapman   Richmond
Surveyor:
William Chadwick
Secretary:
Richard Meade

Appendix B

At the Second General Meeting of the Richmond Railway Company, on 10 February 1846, and at which minutes were taken, the following are listed as Directors, in the order shown:

W. Chadwick (Chairman)   E. Chapman
Count Eyre   T. Long
W. Knott   J.D. Lowden
W. Bland   C.R. Whiting
T.B. Simpson (Deputy Chairman)   V.D. Salomons

At this meeting W. Bland resigned, and elected to his vacancy was Benjamin Edgington of Duke Street.

The following are listed as Shareholders, in the order shown:

I. Crawford	F. Ashby	J. Massey	I. Buckmaster
I. Grant	T. Twining	T.H. Massey	I.A. Chowne
T. Twining Jnr	P.R. Larton	J. Hibbert, Jnr	H. Pearson
G. Gwilt	C.O. Apperley	F.C. Finch	A. Wilcoxan
I. Jackson	A. Inderwick	Ch. Hill	I. Hibbert
T. Chadwick	C. Stevens	S. Wreford	T. Ashton

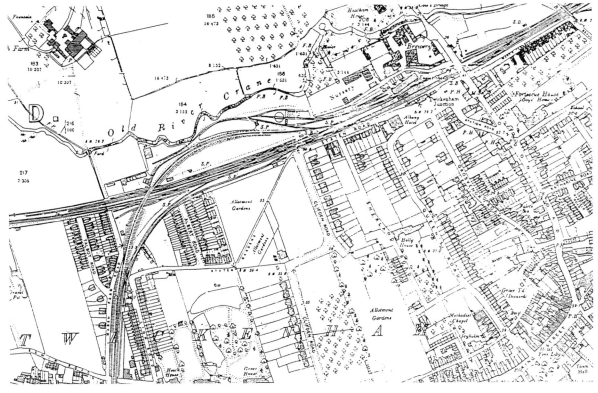

Twickenham in the 1890's.

Appendix C – Rights of Way

The railway from Barnes to Richmond crossed several roads and paths, and it was thus a problem for residents who needed to cross it, and a problem for the railway operators who needed to keep them off the line. For example the Richmond Railway Act of 1845 empowered the Company to stop up Church Path at Mortlake and make a footbridge.

In 1847 an action was brought against the Company for stopping up another path, but this was settled by Church Path bridge being taken down and the path opened up again.

In 1886 the LSWR put the bridge up again for safety reasons, and in October 1903 the path was stopped up again for the same reason. An action was brought by Barnes Urban District Council to get it opened again. Judgement was in their favour as the Court held that the Company could not stop up the path as they had dedicated it to the public in 1847.

The railway company then introduced a Private Bill in order to get Powers, explaining that traffic had increased on the line from 24 trains per day in 1849 to 14 per hour in 1905. Children were crossing the line and it had been the railway's policy to close the paths.

This comes from an editorial article in the Railway Magazine of August 1906 p.214-5, the outcome not being given. In any event closure of the paths became essential with the advent of third-rail electrification in 1916. There are now concrete footbridges between Mortlake and Sheen.

The legal action referred to above features in the Minutes of Mortlake Vestry, who were also antagonised by the LSWR running trains during the hours of Divine service on Sundays, a problem experienced elsewhere with railways in the 1840s and 1850s. The Bishop of London was asked to intercede on behalf of the Vestry, and the LSWR apologised shifting the blame on to the Richmond Railway, who, they alleged, wanted to increase traffic and the value of the line before selling it.

The overbridge which now carries the South Circular Road was built by the LSWR in 1905 as a condition of sale by Capt Fitzgerald of land for quadrupling the line between Mortlake and Richmond. The writer does not yet know why the quadrupling was not carried out.

Barnes UDC opposed the LSWR 1913 Bill for electrification because they felt there would be more delays at the level crossings (because of more trains). The LSWR agreed to replace the crossings with bridges if this happened, but by 1916 it had not. The LSWR offered to share the cost of bridges at White Hart Lane and Sheen Lane, and to widen Barnes bridge. Apparently this met with no response, as had a proposal in 1901 to Richmond Council to replace Manor Road crossing with a bridge.

Main dates in Richmond railway history

27 July 1846   Richmond to Nine Elms service opened

11 July 1848   Waterloo station opened

22 August 1848   Richmond to Datchet service opened

22 August 1849   Barnes to Isleworth opened

1 December 1849   Datchet to Windsor line opened

1 February 1850   Loop line completed to Feltham

9 July 1856   Reading service started

20 May 1858   North London trains reach Richmond and Twickenham

1 February 1862   Kew curve and Barnes curve opened

2 March 1863   Clapham Junction opened

1 July 1863   Twickenham to Kingston line opened

1 November 1864   Shepperton line opened

1 November 1865   Broad Street station opened

1 January 1869   Richmond 'New' station opened, Kew Gardens station opened, and service to Ludgate Hill via Kensington started

2 October 1876   St Margarets station opened

1 July 1877   District service to Mansion House started

1 October 1877   Metropolitan service to Aldgate started

1 August 1905   Electrification of District Railway

31 December 1906   Metropolitan service withdrawn

30 January 1916   Electrification of Waterloo-Richmond-Kingston and Shepperton services

12 March 1916   Electrification of loop line

4 June 1916   Ludgate Hill via Kensington service withdrawn

1 October 1916   Electrification of North London line

1 August 1937   Opening of re-built station at Richmond

27 March 1963   Beeching Report published

21 June 1965   Proposal to close Broad Street services withdrawn

June 1971   Second closure threat to Broad Street services

13 May 1985   London's newest railway service starts: Richmond-North Woolwich, the 'North London Link'

A selection of Tickets used over the years

LSWR/SR/BR TICKETS TO SOUTHERN DESTINATIONS

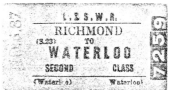

LSWR

SR

SR (Machine Issue)

BR Early Automatic

BTC Season (in SR style)

BOOKINGS TO THE UNDERGROUND

LSWR

**BR (S) Vertical
scheme ticket**

**Station of origin to any
LT station**

**A late development headed
LONDON TRANSPORT though still
with BRB conditions on the back**

BOOKINGS TO OR VIA THE NORTH LONDON LINE

N&SWJR

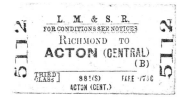

LMS Standard Type

S Reg Print

Headed LMSR (in fact an early BR ticket when it
was decreed that prenationalisation titles were to
be retained for a time).

Time Tables

RICHMOND, TWICKENHAM, KEW AND WINDSOR LINES. — Week-day Trains.

DOWN.

From
WATERLOO BRIDGE
Vauxhall
Wandsworth
Putney
Barnes

Chiswick
Kew
Brentford
Spring Grve. & Isleworth
Hounslow & Whitton
Feltham

Mortlake
RICHMOND
Twickenham

Feltham
Ashford
Staines
Wraysbury
Datchet
WINDSOR

UP.

From
WINDSOR
Datchet
Wraysbury
Staines
Ashford
Feltham
Twickenham
RICHMOND
Mortlake

Feltham
Hounslow & Whitton
Spring Grove & Isleworth
Brentford
Kew
Chiswick

Barnes
Putney
Wandsworth
Vauxhall
WATERLOO BRIDGE

A This is a Third Class Train from Windsor, Wraysbury and Staines to London only.
B This Train will stop at Ashford on Saturdays to set down London Passengers.
C These Trains will stop at Chiswick by Signal only.
D This Train will stop at Wraysbury by Signal, and to set down Passengers who have previously communicated their destination to the Guard.
T This Train will stop at Datchet by Signal.

* OMNIBUSES leave the Spread Eagle, Gracechurch Street, City, half an hour before the departure of these TRAINS from Waterloo Bridge, and on arrival of these Trains marked *
For Trains on Staines, Reading and Wokingham Line, see page 27

Above: Page 28 of the LSWR time table of November 1859.
Below: Richmond in the 1890's.

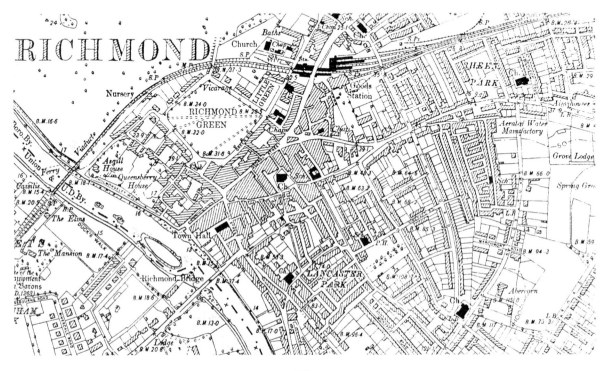

LONDON AND SOUTH WESTERN RAILWAY.

OPENING OF A NEW ROUTE.

LONDON (Waterloo, Ludgate Hill, Moorgate Street, and Metropolitan Stations) to KEW GARDENS and RICHMOND, Via CHELSEA, BROMPTON, KENSINGTON HAMMERSMITH, TURNHAM GREEN, and BRENTFORD ROAD

September, 1869.

WEEK DAYS.

STATIONS.	1 2 3	1 2 3	1 2 3	1 2 3	1 2 3	1 2 3	1 2 3	1 2 3	1 2 3	1 2 3	1 2 3	1 2 3	1 2 3	1 2 3	1 2 3	1 2 3	1 2 3	1 2 3	1 2 3	1 2 3	1 2 3	1 2 3	1 2 3	1 2 3	1 2 3	1 2 3	1 2 3	1 2 3
	a m	a m	a m	a m	a m	a m	a m	a m	a m	a m	a m	p m	p m	p m	p m	p m	p m	p m	p m	p m	p m	p m	p m	p m	p m	p m	p m	p m
Reading ....dep	..	..	..	..	..	..	8 7	..	..	9 0	10 35	..	..	..	..	..	..	1 50	..	..	..	..	4 15	..	..	..	..	7 45
Windsor .... ,,	..	..	..	..	7 55	..	8 50	..	..	10 40	..	11 25	..	..	..	..	..	2 35	..	..	..	..	..	5 30	6 15	..	..	8 30
Shepperton .... ,,	..	..	..	7 45	..	8 35	..	9 30	..	10 55	..	..	..	..	..	1 35	..	..	3 43	3 43	..	..	5 20	..	..	6 55	7 40	..
Kingston .... ,,	..	6 45	7 40	..	8 40	..	9 15	9 45	..	10 45	11 30	..	..	12 50	..	1 50	..	2 55	3 35	3 55	4 35	..	..	5 35	6 48	7 15	8 25	9 30
Twickenham .... ,,	..	6 56	7 51	8 7	8 51	8 58	9 34	9 56	10 2	11 16	11 47	11 56	..	1 1	..	2 1	..	3 14	3 46	4 7	4 48	..	5 42	5 57	7 0	7 26	8 36	9 41
Richmond (O. S.) arr		7 1	7 56	8 12	8 56	9 3	9 39	10 2	10 34	11 21	11 52	12 1	..	1 6	..	2 6		3 19	3 51	4 12	4 53	..	5 47	6 2	7 5	7 31	8 41	9 46
Richmond (New Stn.) dep.	6 53	7 15	8 0	8 15	8 58	9 1[illegible]	10 0	10 15	10 55	11 23	11 55	12 15	12 55	1 15	1 55	2 15	2 55	3 26	4 15	4 25	5 0	5 15	6 0	6 30	7 12	7 35	8 45	9 50
Kew Gardens .... ,,	6 57	7 19	8 4	8 19	9 3	9 20	10 4	10 19	10 59	11 27	11 59	12 19	12 59	1 19	1 59	2 19	2 59	3 30	4 19	4 29	5 4	5 19	6 4	6 34	7 16	7 39	8 49	9 54
Brentford Road .... ,,	7 1	7 24	8 8	8 23	9 7	9 24	10 9	10 2[illegible]	11 3	11 31	12 3	12 23	1 3	1 23	2 3	2 23	3 3	3 34	4 23	4 33	5 8	5 23	6 8	6 38	7 20	7 43	8 53	9 58
Turnham Green .... ,,	7 5	7 27	8 11	8 27	9 10	9 27	10 12	10 26	11 6	11 34	12 6	12 27	1 7	1 26	2 6	2 26	3 6	3 37	4 27	4 36	5 11	5 26	6 11	6 41	7 23	7 46	8 56	10 1
Hammersmith .... arr	7 8	7 30	8 14	8 30	9 13	9 30	10 15	10 30	11 10	11 38	12 10	12 30	1 10	1 30	2 10	2 30	3 10	3 41	4 30	4 39	5 15	5 30	6 15	6 45	7 27	7 50	9 0	10 5
Metro-politan: Hammersmith "A" de.	7 15	7 35	8 20	8 37	9 20	9 37	10 20	10 37	11 15	11 55	12 15	12 35	1 15	1 35	2 15	2 35	3 15	3 52	4 37	4 52	5 20	5 37	6 20	6 55	7 37	7 55	9 15	10 15
Metro-politan: Bishop's Road ,,	7 30	7 50	8 35	8 52	9 35	9 52	10 35	10 52	11 30	12 10	12 30	12 5[illegible]	1 30	1 50	2 30	2 50	3 30	4 10	4 52	5 10	5 35	5 52	6 35	7 10	7 59	8 10	9 30	10 30
Metro-politan: Moorgate Street ,,	7 53	8 14	9 0	9 13	10 0	10 16	11 0	11 16	11 53	12 33	12 53	1 14	1 53	2 14	2 53	3 14	3 53	4 33	5 16	5 33	6 0	6 16	7 0	7 33	8 16	8 33	9 53	10 53
Hammersmith .... dep.	7 9	7 31	8 15	8 31	9 14	9 32	10 17	10 31	11 12	11 30	12 11	12 31	1 12	1 32	2 12	2 31	3 12	3 42	4 31	4 40	5 16	5 31	6 17	6 46	7 28	7 51	9 1	10 6
Kensington .... ,,	7 13	7 36	8 20	8 37	9 18	9 38	10 24	10 37	11 20	11 44	12 17	12 36	1 18	1 40	2 18	2 36	3 20	3 46	4 37	4 46	5 20	5 38	6 24	6 52	7 33	7 58	9 6	10 11
West Brompton .... ,,	7 17	7 39	8 23	8 40	9 21	9 41	10 27	10 40	11 23	11 47	12 20	12 39	1 21	1 43	2 21	2 39	3 23	3 50	4 40	4 49	5 23	5 41	6 27	6 55	7 36	8 1	9 9	10 14
Chelsea .... ,,	7 19	7 41	8 25	8 43	9 23	9 43	10 29	10 42	11 25	11 50	12 22	12 41	1 23	1 45	2 24	2 41	3 25	3 52	4 42	4 51	5 25	5 43	6 29	6 57	7 38	8 3	9 11	10 16
Battersea .... ,,	7 22	7 44	8 28	8 46	9 26	9 6	10 32	10 45	11 28	11 53	12 25	12 44	1 26	1 48	2 27	2 44	3 28	3 53	4 45	4 54	5 28	5 46	6 32	7 0	7 41	8 6	9 14	10 19
Ludgate Hill Line: Wandsworth Road ,,	7 29	..	8 34	..	9 33	..	10 38	..	11 37	..	12 32	..	1 34	..	2 35	..	3 37	..	4 53	..	5 37	..	6 39	..	7 48	..	9 20	..
Ludgate Hill Line: Clapham ,,	7 32	..	8 37	..	9 36	..	10 41	..	11 40	..	12 35	..	1 37	..	2 38	..	3 40	..	4 56	..	5 40	..	6 42	..	7 51	..	9 23	..
Ludgate Hill Line: Brixton ,,	7 35	..	8 40	..	9 39	..	10 44	..	11 43	..	12 38	..	1 40	..	2 41	..	3 43	..	4 59	..	5 43	..	6 45	..	7 54	..	9 26	..
Ludgate Hill Line: Loughboro' Road ,,	7 38	..	8 43	..	9 42	..	10 47	..	11 46	..	12 41	..	1 43	..	2 44	..	3 46	..	5 2	..	5 46	..	6 48	..	7 5	..	9 29	..
Ludgate Hill Line: Camberwell Road ,,	7 41	..	8 46	..		..	10 50	..	11 49	..	12 44	..	1 46	..	2 47	..	3 49	..	5 5	..	5 49	..	6 51	..	8 0	..	9 32	..
Ludgate Hill Line: Walworth Road ,,	7 44	..	..	..	9 46	..	10 53	..	11 52	..	12 47	..	1 49	..	2 50	..	3 52	..	5 8	..	5 52	..	6 54	..	8 3	..	9 35	..
Ludgate Hill Line: Elephant & Castle ,,	7 47	..	..	..	..	..	10 56	..	11 55	..	12 50	..	1 52	..	2 53	..	3 55	..	5 11	..	5 55	..	6 57	..	8 6	..	9 38	..
Ludgate Hill Line: Borough Road ,,		..	..	..		..	10 58	..	11 57	..		..	1 54	..	..	..	3 57	..	5 13	..		..	6 59	..	8 8	..	9 40	..
Ludgate Hill Line: Blackfriars Bridge ,,	7 51	..	8 52	..	9 52	..	11 1	..	12 0	..	12 54	..	1 57	..	2 57	..	4 0	..	5 16	..	5 59	..	7 2	..	8 11	..	9 43	..
Ludgate Hill Line: Ludgate Hill ... arr.	7 53		8 54		9 54		11 3		12 2		12 56		1 59	..	2 59	..	4 2	..	5 18		6 1	..	7 4	..	8 13		9 45	..
Vauxhall .... ,,	..	7 51	..	8 55	..	9 54	..	10 52	..	12 0	..	12 51	..	1 55	..	2 51	..	4 2	..	5 1	..	5 53	..	7 6	..	8 13	..	10 26
Waterloo .... ,,	..	7 58	..	9 2	..	10 1	..	10 59	..	12 7	..	12 58	..	2 2	..	2 58	..	4 9	..	5 8	..	6 0	..	7 13	..	8 20	..	10 33

September, 1869.

SUNDAYS.

STATIONS.	a m	a m	a m	a m	p m	p m	p m	p m	p m	p m	p m	p m	p m	p m	p m	p m	p m	p m	p m	p m	p m	p m	p m	p m	p m	p m	..	..
Reading ....dep.	..	..	..	8 0	..	..	..	..	..	..	..	..	..	..	..	..	..	..	..	..	..	..	..	7 45	..	..	..	..
Windsor .... ,,	..	..	..	8 45	..	..	..	1 45	..	..	..	..	..	..	5 5	6 5	..	..	..	..	..	..	..	..	..	..	..	..
Shepperton .... ,,	..	..	..	..	..	..	..	1 55	..	..	..	..	..	..	4 50	..	..	..	..	..	7 8	..	..	..	9 15	..	..	..
Kingston .... ,,	..	..	8 25	9 0	..	1 12	..	..	..	3 20	..	4 10	..	..	5 5	6 5	..	..	6 50	..	7 20	..	8 30	..	9 10	9 45	..	..
Twickenham .... ,,	..	..	8 39	9 20	..	1 26	..	2 20	..	3 31	..	4 24	..	5 10	5 45	6 19	..	..	7 4	..	7 35	..	8 42	9 6	9 36	9 59	..	..
Richmond (O. S.) arr	..	..	8 44	9 25		1 31	..	2 25	..	3 39	..	4 29	..	5 15	5 50	6 24	..	..	7 9	..	7 40	..	8 47	9 11	9 41	10 4	..	..
Richmond (New Stn.) dep.	7 50	8 30	9 15	9 55	12 50	1 35	1 50	2 35	3 33	3 55	4 10	4 33	4 55	5 30	5 55	6 25	6 30	6 55	7 25	7 30	7 55	8 25	9 0	9 25	9 50	10 25	..	..
Kew Gardens .... ,,	7 55	8 35	9 19	9 59	12 54	1 39	1 55	2 39	3 37	3 59	4 14	4 37	4 59	5 34	5 59	6 29	6 35	6 59	7 29	7 35	7 59	8 29	9 4	9 29	9 54	10 29	..	..
Brentford Road .... ,,	7 59	8 39	9 23	10 3	12 58	1 43	1 59	2 43	3 41	4 3	4 18	4 41	5 3	5 38	6 3	6 33	6 39	7 3	7 33	7 39	8 3	8 33	9 8	9 33	9 59	10 33	..	..
Turnham Green......... ,,	8 3	8 43	9 27	10 7	1 2	1 47	2 3	2 47	3 44	4 7	4 22	4 44	5 7	5 12	6 7	6 37	6 43	7 7	7 37	7 43	8 7	8 37	9 12	9 37	10 3	10 37	..	..
Hammersmith......... arr.	8 7	8 47	9 30	10 10	1 5	1 50	2 7	2 50	3 47	4 10	4 25	4 47	5 10	5 15	6 10	6 40	6 47	7 10	7 40	7 47	8 10	8 40	9 15	9 40	10 6	10 40	..	..
Metro-politan: Hammersmith "A" de.	8 15	8 55	9 35	10 15	1 15	1 55	2 15	2 55	3 55	4 15	4 35	4 55	5 15	5 55	6 15	6 55	6 55	7 15	7 55	7 55	8 15	8 55	9 15	9 55	10 15	10 55	..	..
Metro-politan: Bishop's Road ,,	8 30	9 10	9 50	10 30	1 30	2 10	2 30	3 10	4 10	4 30	4 50	5 10	5 30	6 10	6 30	7 10	7 10	7 30	8 10	8 10	8 30	9 10	9 30	10 10	10 30	11 10	..	..
Metro-politan: Moorgate Street ..arr.	8 53	9 33	10 13	10 53	1 53	2 33	2 53	3 33	4 33	4 53	5 13	5 33	5 53	6 33	6 53	7 33	7 33	7 53	8 33	8 33	8 53	9 33	9 53	10 33	10 53	11 33	..	..
Hammersmith .... dep.	8 8	8 48	9 31	10 11	1 6	1 51	2 8	2 51	3 48	4 11	4 26	4 48	5 11	5 46	6 11	6 41	6 48	7 11	7 41	7 48	8 11	8 41	9 11	9 41	10 7	10 41	..	..
Kensington .... ,,	8 14	8 54	9 37	10 17	1 10	1 57	2 14	2 57	3 54	4 17	4 30	4 54	5 17	5 50	6 17	6 45	6 53	7 17	7 45	7 54	8 17	8 45	9 17	9 45	10 12	10 46	..	..
West Brompton ...... ,,	8 17	8 57	9 40	10 21	1 13	2 0	2 17	3 0	3 57	4 20	..	4 57	5 20	..	6 20	..	6 57	7 20	..	7 57	8 20	..	9 22	..	10 15	10 49	..	..
Chelsea .... ,,	8 19	8 59	9 42	10 24	1 16	2 2	2 19	3 2	3 59	4 22	..	4 59	5 22	..	6 22	..	6 59	7 22	..	7 59	8 22	..	9 23	..	10 18	10 52	..	..
Battersea .... ,,	8 22	9 2	9 45	10 28	1 19	2 5	2 22	3 5	4 2	4 25	..	5 2	5 25	..	6 25	..	7 2	7 25	..	8 2	8 25	..	9 26	..	10 21	10 55	..	..
Ludgate Hill Line: Wandsworth Road ,,	8 29	9 9	..	..	1 25	..	2 29	...	4 9	..	..	5 9	..	..	..	..	7 9	..	..	8 9	..	..	9 29	..	..	..	..	..
Ludgate Hill Line: Clapham ,,	8 32	9 12	..	..	1 28	..	2 32	..	4 12	..	..	5 12		..	..	..	7 12	..	..	8 12	..	..	9 33	..	..	..	..	..
Ludgate Hill Line: Brixton ,,	8 35	9 15	..	..	1 31	..	2 35	..	4 15	..	..	5 15	..	..	..	..	7 15	..	..	8 15	..	..	..	..	..	..	..	..
Ludgate Hill Line: Loughboro' Road ,,	8 38	9 18	...	..	1 34	..	2 38	..	4 18	..	..	5 18	..	..	..	..	7 18	..	..	8 18	..	..	..	..	..	..	..	..
Ludgate Hill Line: Camberwell Road ,,	8 41	9 21	..	..	1 37	..	2 41	..	4 21	..	..	5 21	..	..	..	..	7 21	..	..	8 21	..	..	..	..	..	..	..	..
Ludgate Hill Line: Walworth Road ,,	8 44	9 24	..	..	1 40	..	2 44	..	4 24	..	..	5 24	..	..	..	..	7 24	..	..	8 24	..	..	..	..	..	..	..	..
Ludgate Hill Line: Elephant & Castle ,,	8 47	9 27	..	..	1 43	..	2 47	..	4 27	..	..	5 27	..	..	..	..	7 27	..	..	8 27	..	..	..	..	..	..	..	..
Ludgate Hill Line: Borough Road ,,	8 49	9 29	..	..	1 45	..	2 49	..	4 29		..	5 29	..	..	..	..	7 29	..	..	8 29	..	..	..	..	..	..	..	..
Ludgate Hill Line: Blackfriars Bridge ,,	8 52	9 32	..	..	1 48	..	2 52	..	4 32	..	..	5 32	..	..	..	..	7 32	..	..	8 32	..	..	..	..	..	..	..	..
Ludgate Hill Line: Ludgate Hill ...... arr.	8 54	9 34	..	..	1 50	..	2 54	..	4 34	..	..	5 34	..	..	..	..	7 34	..	..	8 34	..	..	..	..	..	..	..	..
Vauxhall .... ,,	..	..	9 51	10 35	..	2 11	..	3 11	..	4 31	..	..	5 31	..	6 31	..	..	7 31	..	..	8 31	..	9 34	..	10 27	11 1	..	..
Waterloo .... ,,	..	..	9 58	10 42	..	2 18	..	3 18	..	4 38	..	..	5 38	..	6 38	..	..	7 38	..	..	8 38	..	9 41	..	10 34	11 8	..	..

A The Stations between Hammersmith and Moorgate Street are Shepherd's Bush, Notting Hill, Westbourne Park, Bishop's Road, Edgware Road, Baker Street, Portland Road, Gower Street, King's Cross, Farringdon Street, and Aldersgate Street.

Waterloo Junc. Station is now Open, & Trains run every 10 minutes between Waterloo, Cannon St., & Charing Cross Stations.

Richmond Area 1922/3

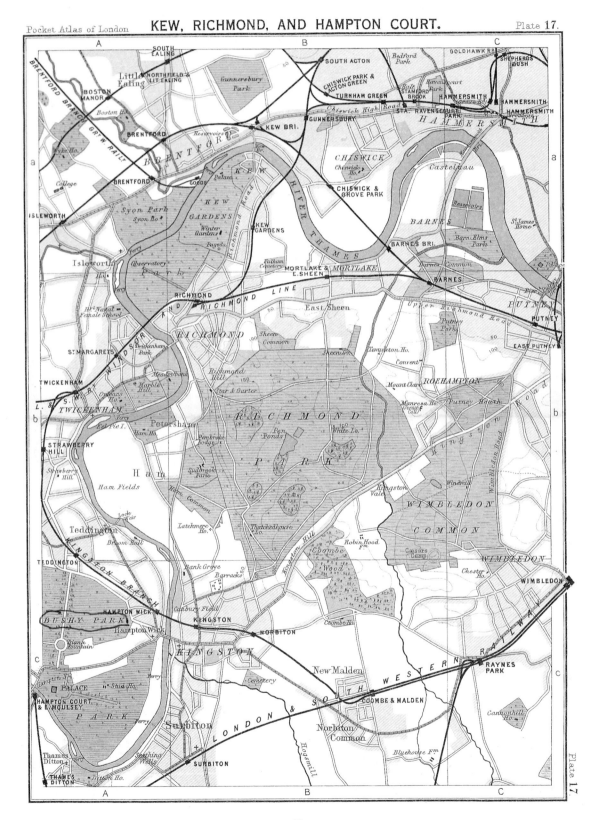

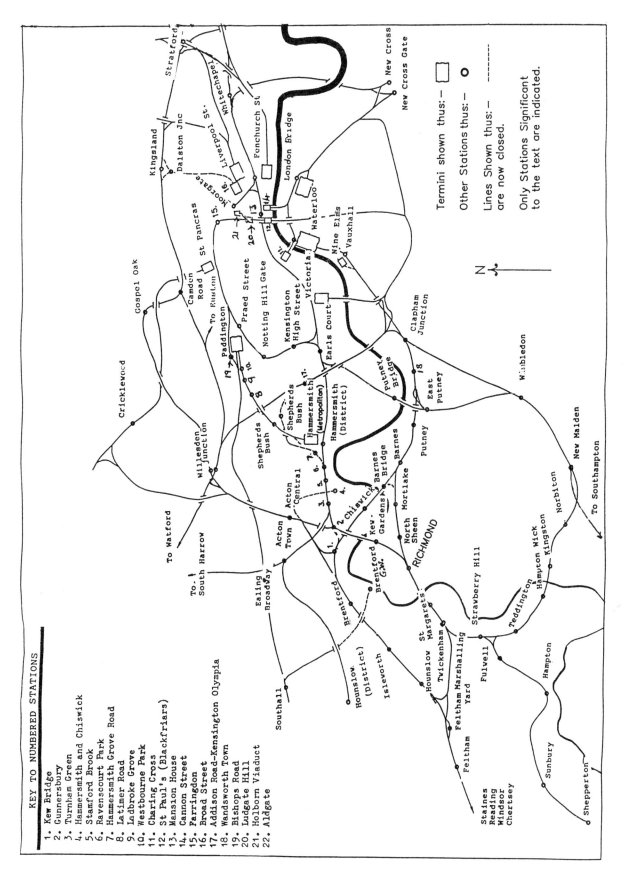

KEY TO NUMBERED STATIONS

1. Kew Bridge
2. Gunnersbury
3. Turnham Green
4. Hammersmith and Chiswick
5. Stanford Brook
6. Ravenscourt Park
7. Hammersmith Grove Road
8. Latimer Road
9. Ladbroke Grove
10. Westbourne Park
11. Charing Cross
12. St Paul's (Blackfriars)
13. Mansion House
14. Cannon Street
15. Farringdon
16. Broad Street
17. Addison Road-Kensington Olympia
18. Wandsworth Town
19. Bishops Road
20. Ludgate Hill
21. Holborn Viaduct
22. Aldgate

Termini shown thus:—

Other Stations thus:— ○

Lines Shown thus:—
are now closed. - - - - -

Only Stations Significant
to the text are indicated.

Bibliography

1. Primary Sources:
a. Minutes of Evidence etc in House of Lords Record Office:
   Richmond Railway Bill 21 July 1845.
   North and South Western Junction Railway Bill 3 June 1851.
   London and South Western Railway (Kensington) Bill 4 March 1864.
   Hammersmith and City Railway Bill 14 March 1864.
   Plan etc. for London and South Western Railway, Kensington and Richmond – deviations and new lines etc. 30 November 1864.
   Amendment to London and South Western Railway (Kensington) Act 1864, 16 March 1865.
b. Company Records in British Transport Historical Records collection in Public Record Office, Kew:
   Prospectus, Richmond and West End Junction Railway (undated)
   Minutes, Board of Directors, Richmond Railway Company.
   Minutes, Court of Directors, London and South Western Railway Company.
   Report from the Board of Trade on schemes for facilitating the approach to the Metropolis 1845.
c. Other contemporaneous records:
   Illustrated London News
   The Builder
   Building News
   The Architect
   Hansard Official Record
   Herepath
   Hiscoke's and Sons Richmond Notes
   Richmond and Twickenham Times
   Richmond Herald
   West London Observer
2. Secondary Sources:
   K. Bailey, Hypothetical History – or some railways that never were. Wandsworth Historian, No. 8, June 1973.
   T. Barker and R.M. Robbins, History of London Transport, vol. 1, 1975, vol. 2, 1976.
   W. Besant, London in the Nineteenth Century, 1909.
   J. Betjeman, First and Last Loves, 1952.
   J. Betjeman, London's Historic Railway Stations, 1978.
   G. Biddle and O.S. Nock, The Railway Heritage of Britain, 1983.
   H.V. Borley and C.E. Lee, The North London Line, Railway Magazine, February 1964.
   B. Cherry and N. Pevsner, The Buildings of England, London 2: South, 1983.
   E. Course, London Railways, 1962.
   D. Edwards and R. Pigram, The Golden Years of the Metropolitan Railway, 1983.
   J.C. Gillham, The Railways of Kew and Gunnersbury, Railway Magazine, September 1956.
   A.A. Jackson, London's Termini, 1972.
   A.A. Jackson, London's Local Railways, 1978.
   A.A. Jackson, London's Metropolitan Railway, 1986.
   G.M. Kerr, Trans Thames to Richmond, Railway Magazine, August 1980, September 1980.
   R.W. Kidner, Southern Suburban Steam 1860-1967, 1984.
   E. Klapper, London's Lost Railways, 1976.

C.E. Lee, The Metropolitan District Railway, 1963.

G.T. Moody, Southern Electric 1909-1979, 1979.

National Railway Museum, North London Railway – a pictorial record, 1979.

G.A. Pryer, Track Layout Diagrams of the Southern Railway, Section 8, Windsor Lines, 1984.

R.M. Robbins, Points and Signals, 1969.

R.M. Robbins, The North London Railway, 1983.

T. Sherwood, The London and South Western Railway 1837-1856, Wandsworth Historian No.42, September 1984.

T. Sherwood, Why Clapham Junction? Railway Magazine, August 1986.

J. Simmons, The Railways of Britain, edn. 1968.

J. Simmons, The Railway in England and Wales 1830-1914, 1978.

J. Simmons, The Railway in Town and Country, 1986.

R. Thorne, Environs of London, 1876.

E. Walford, Greater London, vol.1 n.d.

H.P. White, London Railway History (vol. 3 of Regional History of the Railways of Great Britain), 1971.

H.P. White, Southern England (vol. 2 of Regional History of the Railways of Great Britain), 1982.

R.A. Williams, London and South Western Railway, vol. 1, 1968; vol. 2, 1973.

ACKNOWLEDGEMENTS

I would like to thank the staff of the Local Studies Library at Richmond, The Local Studies Library at Twickenham, the staff of the House of Lords Record Office, The Public Records Office (Kew), and Mr Reg Randell of British Rail. Also Mr Chris Austin of British Rail, and Mr Terry Turbin, Curator, North Woolwich Station Museum.

My friend John Smith M.Phil. read the draft manuscript, and I would like to thank him for his comments. Any errors, however, are entirely my responsibility.

ILLUSTRATIONS

The author and publishers wish to thank and acknowledge the following:

British Rail Architects Department p56 (middle and bottom)

Collection H.J. Patterson Rutherford p28 (top)

Len's of Sutton p17 (bottom left), p18 (top and centre), p28 (centre left) pp33 and 45

Brian Morrison p23 (bottom), p46 (middle)

Richmond Public Libraries pp5, 8 and 9

Douglas Stuckey p18 (bottom right), p35, p38 (centre and bottom) p55 (centre and bottom), p56 (top)

C.F.D. Whetmath p38 (top), p46 (bottom), p55 (top)

Particulars of tickets were kindly provided by John Shelbourn of the Transport Ticket Society.

Other modes of Transport

The first steamboat arriving at Richmond.

'The last Omnibus' at Richmond in May 1847.